The Meaning of
TAROT

The Meaning of
TAROT

DAVID HOY

Aurora Publishers, Inc.
Nashville/London

COPYRIGHT © 1971 BY
AURORA PUBLISHERS INCORPORATED
NASHVILLE, TENNESSEE 37219
LIBRARY OF CONGRESS CATALOG CARD NUMBER: 79-128449
STANDARD BOOK NUMBER: 87695-073-X
MANUFACTURED IN THE UNITED STATES OF AMERICA

I am deeply indebted to RON DECKARD, *scholarly gentleman, versatile composer, and fabulous friend, for his help in researching and writing this manuscript on the Tarot.*

Acknowledgments

Research for *The Meaning of Tarot* required the immense cooperation of several people, and I want to express my deep debt of gratitude to these people.

I want to especially thank Ron Deckard for closeting himself in several university libraries to dig out the little-known history and background of Tarot.

I also want to acknowledge the splendid cooperation of Dr. Spencer P. Thornton, not only for his research but also for his years of deepening friendship and his continued encouragement as I continue my work in all phases of occult lore and esoteric wisdom.

My commendation also goes to artist Dale Phillips for his contribution in portraying the depth of meaning contained in the hundreds of symbols incorporated into the deck of Tarot cards. His mental prowess in "divining" exactly what I was after in the visible expression of Tarot is inspiring.

David Hoy

Contents

PART ONE: WHAT IS THE TAROT? 1

PART TWO: ORIGIN OF THE TAROT 7

PART THREE: PRELIMINARY TO THE
    DIVINATORY READING 19

  TRAINING THE SUBCONSCIOUS MIND 28
  WHEN TO READ THE CARDS 29
  WHERE TO SPREAD THE CARDS 30
  WHERE TO READ THE CARDS 31
  WHO SHOULD BE PRESENT 32
  WHERE TO SIT 32
  READING FOR YOURSELF OR FOR ABSENT
    INQUIRERS 33
  NATURE OF THE PRELIMINARY CONVERSATION 33
  PINPOINTING THE INQUIRY 34
  SELECTING THE SPREAD 35
  SHUFFLING AND CUTTING 36
  SPREADING THE CARDS 39
  READING THE CARDS 39
  UNSATISFACTORY READINGS 41

PART FOUR: METHODS OF DIVINATION 43

  PYRAMID SPREAD 47
  THREE SEVENS SPREAD 48
  SPREAD OF 35 50
  SPREAD OF 36 52
  HORSESHOE SPREAD 54
  PERSONAL HOROSCOPE SPREAD 56
  YES OR NO SPREAD 60

TREE OF LIFE SPREAD	62
ANCIENT CELTIC SPREAD	66
VICTORY CROSS SPREAD	70

PART FIVE: THE MAJOR ARCANA 71

ARCANUM I	THE MAGICIAN	75
ARCANUM II	THE HIGH PRIESTESS	77
ARCANUM III	THE EMPRESS	82
ARCANUM IV	THE EMPEROR	85
ARCANUM V	THE HIEROPHANT	88
ARCANUM VI	THE LOVERS	92
ARCANUMN VII	THE CHARIOT	95
ARCANUM VIII	JUSTICE	97
ARCANUM IX	THE HERMIT	99
ARCANUM X	THE WHEEL OF FORTUNE	101
ARCANUM XI	STRENGTH	103
ARCANUM XII	THE HANGED MAN	105
ARCANUM XIII	DEATH	107
ARCANUM XIV	TEMPERANCE	109
ARCANUM XV	THE DEVIL	111
ARCANUM XVI	THE TOWER	113
ARCANUM XVII	THE STAR	115
ARCANUM XVIII	THE MOON	117
ARCANUM XIX	THE SUN	119
ARCANUM XX	JUDGMENT	121
ARCANUM XXI	THE FOOL	123
ARCANUM XXII	THE UNIVERSE	128

PART SIX: THE MINOR ARCANA 131

WANDS	135
CUPS	143
SWORDS	151
PENTACLES	158

Part One

What is the Tarot?

OUTWARDLY, the Tarot is a deck of seventy-eight cards, decorated with strange-looking pictures. But the Tarot is more than just a pack of playing cards. Properly the Tarot is a system of thought and a method of divining the past, the present, and the future.

The Tarot has been called the oldest book known to man. This book communicates not with words, but with the more secretive methods of emblematic symbols and images. Indeed, it may be that the deepest secrets of the Tarot cannot be put into words. And its teaching has affected the thinking of men in many cultures throughout the ages of human existence.

Whether the Tarot represents a common origin of the world's chief symbolic philosophical doctrines and occult traditions, or only a synthesis of them, is not known. Whichever it is, the Tarot shows a complex unity or ontological system summing up such diverse studies as numerology, geometrics, astrology, mythology, and theosophy. Furthermore, the Tarot contains the same basic views found in every ancient religion and philosophy, including

THE MEANING OF TAROT

those found in the Old Testament, in old Roman traditions, in ancient Greek mythology, in Druidic legends, and in Hindu epics.

So the Tarot is the ancient occult science, religion, and philosophy of the world of ideas and principles. The Tarot is a monument of human and spiritual thought.

The Tarot symbolically presents universal ideas that are hidden within the human minds of even ordinary men, but are recognized by only an "enlightened few." The Tarot can search into the soul of every man and provide him with an answer to his problems. It is a "mirror" that reflects everything taking place in the universe. Hence, it is the most ancient and most valuable of the instruments of divination.

The word *Tarot* is the French form of an earlier derivative and rhymes with pharaoh, while a variant form, *Tarots*, rhymes with carrots. The Tarot deck consists of seventy-eight cards divided into two parts. The first cards, numbered in Roman numerals from I through XXII, make up what is known as the Major Arcana. The remaining fifty-six cards comprise the Minor Arcana and are separated into four suits having fourteen cards each.

At first sight, these cards appear very strange. But upon closer examination you will notice that the suits of the Minor Arcana resemble the suits of ordinary playing cards, which owe their origin to the Tarot. There are indications that the Major Arcana originally may have been a separate deck, to which the Minor Arcana was added as a symbolic index, so as to give more depth to divinatory readings.

After its widescale introduction into Europe during the Middle Ages, the Tarot became the greatest means of divination in the civilized world, and was regarded almost

What is the Tarot?

as a science in many circles. Gradually, some of the great kings of France, as well as philosophers, mathematicians, scientists, and other learned men, began to use the Tarot to explore the mysteries of life and to guide their people.

Empress Josephine, mistress of Napoleon Bonaparte, frequently consulted a card reader by letter as well as in person. She and other high-ranking contemporaries in Paris held this reader, Mademoiselle Le Normand, in high esteem. It was reported that this famous prophetess accurately predicted the execution of a ruler of Naples and the crowning of a Swedish king.

Even in more recent times, some of the world's great minds have been inspired or influenced by the Tarot. Winston Churchill studied the Tarot to uncover its hidden secrets. Albert Einstein, a great believer in the power of the human mind, studied the Tarot to penetrate its deepest areas. The author and psychic researcher Aldous Huxley also found in the symbols and images of the Tarot new insight into the potential of the human mind. The movie actor Vincent Price is a student of the Tarot who believes that the events of the future can be foreseen in the cards and that present problems can be overcome by applying the wisdom of the Tarot.

But these men are not alone in their deep respect for the symbols and images of the Tarot and its connection with the subconscious activities of the mind. Many great thinkers have looked upon the Tarot with the same respect and consider it to be more than just another instrument of divination. These poets, authors, psychologists, scientists, and religious thinkers have all found a deeper philosophical challenge in the Tarot symbolism and imagery. Some writings that mention the Tarot

THE MEANING OF TAROT

are T. S. Eliot's *The Waste Land*, William Lindsay Gresham's *Nightmare Alley*, P. D. Ouspensky's *A New Model of the Universe*, Charles Williams' *The Greater Trumps*, and Albert Pike's *Morals and the Dogma of the Scottish Rites*. Another famous poet, W. B. Yeats, was a member of a secret brotherhood that dealt with the occult traditions of the Tarot. And followers of the eminent psychoanalyst C. G. Jung consider certain symbols in the Tarot to be blueprints of the unconscious mind.

Most of us are at sometime in our lives interested in either knowing what the future holds or in seeking information dealing with the past or even with the present. Any means unavilable to the ordinary senses would be classified as divination. The use of the Tarot combines our senses and the mystique of the occult to give us this needed and useful information.

Part Two

Origin of the Tarot

No one knows for certain how the Tarots and playing cards in general originated, or who invented them. There has been much speculation on the subject, but we may never learn the answer. Many scholars from various European nations claimed that their country was the first to have the Tarot cards.

One well-established fact, however, is that the Tarots were the first known cards in Europe, although the name varied somewhat in the different countries. Among the many novelties of the Orient that the Crusaders brought back to Europe from the East were Tarot cards. At about the same time, Gypsies began to wander throughout the European countries. Wherever they went, the Gypsies introduced Tarot cards for divining the future. When the Crusaders discovered that the Tarot could be adapted to gambling, they introduced the cards to every capital of Europe; soon, each country began to develop its own national version of the Tarot cards. These packs are the ancestors of the packs of playing cards in use today.

So when you examine the dates and other evidence

THE MEANING OF TAROT

offered by each European country as proof that the Tarots originated in that country, you will find that they appeared in France, Italy, Germany, Spain, and England at just about the same time, and all seem to have originated from some common source outside Europe. Whether they were first brought to Europe and made popular by the Crusaders, the Gypsies, or both, the Tarot cards spread over all the civilized world during the Middle Ages.

The Tarot pack painted in 1393 for King Charles VI of France is the earliest known of the European Tarot cards. In 1392, the king began to feel the first signs of approaching madness; these cards were painted to cheer and amuse him during his illness. What is supposed to be a part of this pack is now in the Cabinet des Estampes in Paris. No one knows today what the draftsman used as a model for these cards.

The king's Tarot cards are delicately painted to resemble the manner in which manuscripts were decorated at that time. Dots were impressed on the golden backgrounds of the cards, forming an ornamental pattern. A silver border frames each picture. A spiral ribbon of small holes embellishes the borders of the cards. This dotted line of holes is technically called a *tare* in the French language. For this reason some scholars think that the name Tarots is derived from these tares.

Although 1393 is the earliest date attributed to a European Tarot pack, the history of the Tarot reaches farther back into the dark pages of antiquity and probably predates the printed word. Many examples could be given that indicate an early knowledge of the Tarot. But, judging from various writings, as time went on the people of

Origin of the Tarot

the ancient world must have become less familiar with the Tarot.

One interesting story of the Tarot's origin claims that the priests of Atlantis knew their continent was going to be destroyed by a flood. In order to preserve their wisdom they sent their adepts to all parts of the earth. Thereafter, these adepts met once a year at the city of Fez in Northwest Africa (Morocco) to exchange knowledge. But following the division of tongues related in the story of Genesis (11:4-9, concerning the Tower of Babel in Babylon) there was a need for a common means of communication at the annual meetings. So the Tarot was designed in symbolic pictures to serve as a means of preserving and communicating the wisdom of the enlightened priesthood of Atlantis.

Another variation of the story claims that after the city of Alexandria in Egypt was destroyed, the city of Fez became the intellectual capital of the world. Just as we have our international conventions today, wise men of that era traveled from all parts of the earth to meet and discuss important matters at Fez. Since there were many different language groups represented at these meetings, the participants tried to create a universal language that would enable them to communicate directly with one another. This new language was embodied in a book consisting of picture cards filled with mystic symbols. This book was the Major Arcana of the Tarot and was used to preserve the teachings of the ancients for all generations, as a common link with all physical and occult sciences.

According to mystic tradition, there is a connection between the Tarot and the legendary Holy Grail. The

THE MEANING OF TAROT

records of this connection are secretly kept in Europe. The four great symbols of the Holy Grail are the Cup, the Sword, the Lance, and the Dish. Similar symbols are used for the four suits of the Tarot Minor Arcana. The symbols of the Tarot suits are as follows:

1. The Cup is the same as the Cup in the Grail legend and corresponds to hearts in common playing cards.
2. The Sword is the same as the Sword in the Grail legend and corresponds to spades in common playing cards.
3. The Wand is the same as the Lance in the Grail legend and corresponds to diamonds in common playing cards.
4. The Pentacle is the same as the Dish in the Grail legend and corresponds to clubs in common playing cards.

It should be explained here that, in the Tarot descriptions, the Wand is sometimes used as a scepter, but was originally a spear or lance before it was refined as a separate entity. In modern playing cards the suit of diamonds is named after the diamond-shaped head of the spear or lance. The emblem of the Tarot Pentacle is really a circle (or dish) containing a pentacle with five angles (a star) or five flanges (five-leaf clover). For some reason the Tarot suit came to be called after the emblem on the dish rather than the dish itself. In common playing cards the clover came to have only three leaves.

The writings of Ezekiel and Daniel show that these prophets had some knowledge of the Tarot, and the New

Origin of the Tarot

Testament Apocalypse, or the Book of Revelation, closely parallels the Tarot. Each of the twenty-two chapters of the Revelation of John deals with the same prophetic symbols as the twenty-two cards of the Tarot Major Arcana. The Books of Moses indicate that the Old Testament Israelites consulted some form of the Tarot upon command from God.

Some schools of thought even doubt that a complete knowledge of the Bible is possible without a thorough knowledge of the Tarot. This is because many parts of the Old Testament are incomprehensible, they claim, without knowledge of the mysteries contained in the Cabala which, in turn, is interpreted by the Tarot.

Another theory has it that the ancient masons of Chaldea used their psychic senses to build a spiritual science. And for some one thousand five hundred years they specialized in astrology and kept records of the information they received concerning the soul of man. Today, the British Museum of Natural History is the home of this ancient record known as the *Anu-Enlil Series of Chaldea*.

Astrology to these ancient masons was not only an accurate means of divination, but also the science of the soul and the key to understanding man and the universe. They used a symbol to mark each of their discoveries and engraved its esoteric interpretation on a separate tablet. The Egyptians called these tablets the Royal Path of Life. The Egyptian word for path is *Tar*, and *Ro*, *Ros*, or *Rog* is royal. The same symbolism found on the tablets decorates the Egyptian Tarot cards.

These ancient tablets have also been called *A-Rosh*. The *A* stands for learning and *Rosh* is the Egyptian name

THE MEANING OF TAROT

for the god Hermes. When a T is placed in front of *A-Rosh*, it becomes *Tarosh*, which means "pictures of Hermes' doctrine." For centuries the Tarot has been called the Ancient Egyptian Tarot. This fact lends credibility to the use of Hermes' name in connection with the Tarot. Another title sometimes thought to be synonymous with the Ancient Egyptian Tarot is The Book of Thoth, or the Golden Book of Hermes, although the latter wording is less well known. Some scholars ascribe the Tarot's origin to Hermes under the two titles just mentioned.

Hermes, entitled *Trismegistus*, "thrice greatest," was the Greek god known as Mercury to the Romans, Nebo to the Babylonians and Rosh to the Egyptians.

According to hermetic tradition, a tunnel under the paws of the Sphinx leads to the subterranean initiatory temple of the Great Pyramid. Within this initiation chamber is an undiscovered record of astrology and the Tarot. Tablets with paintings depicting the teachings of the Tarot are arranged on columns in two rows, one on each side of a passageway. Such an arrangement would allow the initiates to read the pictures in pairs.

According to legend, just before Egypt was invaded and conquered by the armies of the Persian king, the whole initiatory wisdom of ancient Egypt was preserved by recording it in the symbols of Tarot cards. These cards were made of metal or strong leather and were soon used for gambling by the Egyptians. Then the conquering Persians took up the game and throughout subsequent ages transmitted the most sacred and secret wisdom of the ancient Magi.

One of the most interesting theories of the Tarot's origin involves the Gypsies. According to some historians

Origin of the Tarot

of Gypsy history, these wandering people descended from the three sons of Noah and divided into three classes: the Azth, who were shepherds and farmers; the Bodhas, who were magicians; and the Neydes, who were metal workers. These people formed a primitive cult of physical phenomena and worshiped night, day, the moon, the sun, fire, air, water, and all of nature. From this primitive worship of nature came the symbolical Tarot cards and all the nations of the world.

Legend has it that the Gypsies were the original initiates of the temple of Thoth, and that they were the ones who carried the Tarot cards as a means of divination throughout Europe. The Gypsies claim that their own brand of Tarot cards is the oldest book of prophecy in the world and that their people have carried these cards with them ever since they set out from their original home in India untold centuries ago. According to this Gypsy legend, after the ancient Gypsies left India they lived alternately in Persia, Chaldea, Palestine, and Egypt. During the time of Jesus, some of these Gypsy tribes crossed the Black Sea from Palestine into Greece, the Roman Empire, and Vienne in Provence. By this reckoning, the Gypsies brought the Tarot with them to Europe in the first century. For some reason, however, the cards seem to have been a secret of the Gypsies in Europe until the large Gypsy bands from Peloponnesus dispersed throughout the continent in 1417. About that time, too, the Crusaders were spreading the popularity of the Tarot as a gambling device throughout Europe.

This Gypsy legend is not without some facts to support it. There was, for example, a well-established Gypsy barony on the island of Corfu in the fourteenth century.

THE MEANING OF TAROT

And isolated references to the wanderers appeared in Byzantine and Romanian writings of the Middle Ages, but it was not until 1417 that Europeans began to take notice of Gypsies.

The Gypsy language itself is prima-facie evidence of the Gypsy's original connection with Mother India. Their Romany language is definitely an Indian dialect related to Sanskrit. And the abundance of Indian words used in connection with the Tarot cards in Europe indicate that it was introduced in that continent by a race speaking an Indian dialect. The Gypsies themselves claim that the Tarot is the Book of Wisdom of the Romanichals (or Gypsies), the only surviving history of the wandering people who speak an Indian dialect known as Romany.

All of these accounts of the Tarot's origin prove only one thing; no one knows for certain where Tarot originated or with whom. In general, however, all of these accounts credit the Tarot with the same universal and profound purpose. Hence, none of the accounts can be denied entirely. A thorough study of the Tarot reveals that it is linked with much of the teachings of the Hebrew Cabala, and with Egyptian and Babylonian mythology, as well as with much of the ancient Hindu philosophy. In addition, it is common knowledge that for centuries the Gypsies have possessed a mysterious gift for reading the past, the present, and the future by means of the Tarot cards. In conclusion, it is probably safe to presume that the Tarot represents some ancient link, which bridges all the world's great religio-philosophical systems.

The Tarot has been around for a long time, and it is understandable that a certain amount of lore has grown up around the cards. Legends and mysteries have been

Origin of the Tarot

added to the Tarot by the initiates through the years.

In addition to this growth and change, the Tarot has been surrounded by some outside guessing, superstition, and pure myth. And yet, an indestructible and irreducible wisdom remains above all the legends and theories to inspire and reward the earnest seeker of truth and wisdom. No period in man's history has been without seers and prophets to unlock the universal truths contained in the Tarot.

Part Three

Preliminary to the Divinatory Reading

THE Tarot, as we have seen, is sacred to some schools of religious and philosophical thought. It has even been referred to as the bible of astrology. Some teachers of astrological-occult subjects claim that in the shadow of the pyramids the high priests of ancient Egypt used the Tarot cards to foretell the wonders of the future. They supposedly learned the secrets of reading and interpreting the Tarot from the stars. The cards were reputed to have strange and mysterious powers, which for centuries were known only to magicians, alchemists, and seers.

Whether it is magical and sacred or not, when used correctly the Tarot is one of the most famous, ancient, and accurate methods of telling the future, and this has been attested to for centuries.

Skeptics claim there is no more truth to be found in reading the Tarot than in seeking mysterious answers from leaves at the bottom of a cup. Agnostics, on the other hand, admit there may be something to claims of foretelling the future, but they think the cards themselves are props for the Tarot reader, just as a crystal ball is to

THE MEANING OF TAROT

a crystal gazer, or the lines of the hand are to a palmist. These agnostics contend that the active agent is the individual reader's own intuition. They do not believe that the Tarot cards contain strange and wonderful powers that can foretell the future. Furthermore, some psychics maintain that gifted Tarot readers are "made, not born," and that the Tarot divinatory system can be *taught:* but whether it can then be applied by the students with any success depends upon the degree of their own intuitive abilities to "see" into the future.

Now we have mentioned those who are nonbelievers, those who think the Tarot is magical or divine, and those who feel the cards are only props for clairvoyants. Who is right? In answer to the nonbelievers, not only is the Tarot one of the oldest and most accurate methods of telling the future, but the Tarot also has been consulted with success by some of the great personalities of history. Nevertheless, the actual workings of the Tarot appear to lie somewhere between the prop theory and the mysterious properties theory.

A good deal of the art of Tarot divination probably does rely more on the skill and insight of the individual reader than in the magical properties of the cards themselves. But this does not mean that the reader deals the cards into a spread and then interprets those cards arbitrarily to match his insights into the inquirer's situation. For each card in the Tarot deck there is a traditional divinatory meaning that must be read as it is and never changed to fit a particular situation.

Furthermore, the particular cards that make up a spread and their positions in that spread are never prearranged by the reader. Any psychic impressions he receives at

Preliminary to the Divinatory Reading

the outset from the inquirer must later be reflected somehow in the cards, without direct control or manipulation. The only conjectural consideration allowed to the reader is the type of layout or *spread* he feels best relates to the particular subject of inquiry.

After he has chosen the appropriate spread, the reader shuffles all seventy-eight cards, and the inquirer cuts them. Then the reader draws a specified number of cards, one at a time, face down from the top of the deck and lays them out in the traditional position sequence of the spread. At no time during these proceedings does the reader pick through the cards to select ones whose meanings will confirm his previous impressions. To the contrary, his impressions were subliminally passed on to the appropriate cards before they were shuffled and cut.

To illustrate this point, suppose the reader subconsciously "tunes in" on the inquirer's future before the seventy-eight cards are shuffled. Subsequently the cards are shuffled and cut. Then the top fifteen cards are spread face down on the table in an appropriate spread. Now the reader has to use those fifteen cards, as they are positioned, to interpret his initial intuitive impression. But suppose the divinatory meanings of the fifteen cards as positioned in the spread, which also may have a bearing on the reading, do not correlate with his insights? You may think it easy enough for the reader to read whatever he wants, including the details of his insights, into those or any other fifteen cards. But considering that each card has a particular, predetermined meaning, often affected by its position in the spread, it passes the point of "loose" interpretation, especially when we consider

THE MEANING OF TAROT

that there are seven million mathematically possible variations in a fifteen-card spread. If the reader subconsciously foresaw a divorce for the inquirer previous to the shuffle, cut, and spreading of the specified amount of top cards, a divorce card would have to appear in a certain position among the cards in the spread if it were accurately to reflect the reader's initial intuition.

From all this we gather that the Tarot cards are more than mere props; they somehow respond to the influences of the individual psychic center. The beginning student of the Tarot should not be discouraged by this point. There is plenty of evidence to indicate that everyone has at least latent psychic ability, which needs only to be awakened and developed to function on a substantial level. The ensuing material of this chapter should give you an idea of *how* to release your psychic powers.

Although modern knowledge of the natural laws and processes of matter and energy has shed light on how the mystery of the Tarot works, the ritual of preparing the cards for divination has followed these same principles throughout the centuries. It is therefore imperative that the Tarot be handled in a special manner, according to this tradition. This is no mere formality; it is based upon scientific principles of radiation and vibrations.

Hence, the first consideration in handling and subsequently reading the Tarot cards effectively is an understanding of the basic principles of radiation. A term used in physics, radiation is the emission and diffusion of energy from some source in the form of vibrations (or waves), rays, or mere impulses of thought emanations, heat, light, electricity and magnetism (including human magnetism), sounds, etc. Pierre Prévost's theory of ex-

Preliminary to the Divinatory Reading

changes states that everything that exists is simultaneously and continuously losing vibrations through radiation. This means that all substances consisting of matter, whether solid, liquid, or gaseous, tangible or intangible, animate or inanimate—such as rocks, metal, water, air, the brain and nervous system, and human bodies—constantly radiate vibrations that are, in turn, either absorbed or bounced off the other objects around them. Therefore, according to this established law of physics, even the characteristics of magnetism from the human body and thought emanations from the brain are communicated to inanimate objects such as the Tarot cards.

By this time you should be developing an appreciation of how the Tarot cards fall into their proper places in a divinatory spread, considering the reader has sufficiently developed his psychic ability. His intuitive vibrations work as "computer-impulses" in selecting the appropriate cards for an individual reading.

Since you may be the reader, that is, the one who uses the Tarot cards to give divinatory readings for yourself and your friends, it is important that you protect the cards from vibrations other than your own. Never let other people use or even handle your cards, except during a reading when the inquirer, that is, the person for whom the reading is given, must touch them. When you alone handle the cards they are saturated with your own personal magnetism and will subsequently respond to your vibrations. Thus a rapport is formed between the natural vibrations of the cards and the "psychic center" in your mind. Extraneous vibrations continued over a period of time tend to interfere with this rapport and thereby alter the responses of the card to your psychic impressions.

THE MEANING OF TAROT

During a reading the cards are spread on a Tarot board, thereby exposing them to other vibrations in the room. This need not be a cause for concern; it takes a longer time than allowed in individual readings to saturate the cards with the other vibrations present in the room, or for that matter, with the vibrations of the inquirer. That is why a new deck of cards does not respond as easily to the reader's vibratory influences as a deck that has been used for a long time. The cards respond more readily as they become adequately charged with the reader's personal magnetism. The association between the vibrations of the cards and the reader's subconscious becomes stronger as he continues to use his cards. Hence, the more you, as the reader, handle your cards, the more accurate your readings will be.

To protect your cards from foreign vibrations when not in use requires special care. Once the Tarot has been sensitized with your own vibrations, it is wise to exclude the vibrations of other people or objects by wrapping the pack in soft velvet or silk of a deep purple color. Purple is at the dark end of the color spectrum and therefore readily absorbs vibrations. Thus the psychic color of purple cleanses the Tarot of the reader's past impressions during storage and stands as an absorbing barrier to outside vibrations. Nevertheless, the Tarot retains enough of the reader's magnetism to remain "tuned" to his vibratory frequency.

As a further aid to sealing out undesirable vibrations, the wrapped cards should be placed in an unpainted and unvarnished box made of white pine, which is a poor conductor of vibratory energy. The natural vibrations of wood from a healthy tree should not disturb either the

Preliminary to the Divinatory Reading

natural or the sensitized vibrations of the cards, because wood is likely to retain the harmony with nature it shared when it was a living tree.

You may want to keep two Tarot decks, one for divination and one for spiritual enlightenment or philosophical studies. But always store them separately in two different boxes.

One last precaution against the subtle absorption of discordant vibrations: You should store your Tarot box near personal belongings that would likely have been sensitized to your vibrations. If you leave the Tarot box just anywhere around the house or store it near objects that come in close daily contact with other people, the cards will absorb a mixture of vibrations that will interfere with your readings.

THE MEANING OF TAROT

TRAINING THE SUBCONSCIOUS MIND

It is important for the serious Tarot reader to train his subconscious mind. The subconscious is subjected at all times to physical and mental stimulation that tends to disrupt or alter concentrated patterns of thought. The subconscious is pliable and therefore easily affected by each thought or idea it receives. But it never questions these thoughts and ideas; it just responds to their message. Therefore, the mind should be trained to direct its thinking and to induce desired emotions. This is a real art, but it can and must be achieved so that the mind will not "tune in" on irrelevant material during a reading. If you use strong will power and give the subconscious firm orders, the result will be the required rapport between your mind, the Tarot cards, and the mind of the inquirer.

Having a systematic approach to the reading and using the same procedures during each session trains the subconscious to *know* what it is expected to do. This means that the reader must come to the Tarot board in a serious and receptive attitude of concentration each time a reading is to be given. Then, when he is ready to proceed, he should follow the same ritual in defining the questions to be asked, selecting the proper spread, shuffling and cutting the cards himself, or having it done if that is the method he regularly uses.

Following the same procedure each reading helps the mind and "psychic senses" to learn exactly how the cards are to be handled and thereby develops highly skilled habits in the routine. Once they attain this level of development, the mind and "psychic senses" are alert and work smoothly in transforming the impressions they receive into intramuscular activity. The energy generated by these subtle muscular vibrations is channeled through the fingertips to influence the selection of the proper cards and subsequently their arrangement in the spread. The way is then paved for an accurate reading. The rest is up to the reader's ability to interpret the meanings of the card.

WHEN TO READ THE CARDS

There has been much discussion and controversy as to when is the best time to read the cards. Tradition holds Fridays and Mondays as lucky days for card reading. Mademoiselle Le Normand, the famous French cartomancer, thought Fridays were the best days to read the cards, but others maintain that Mondays are better. Some readers claim that certain hours are more favorable than others. This may be a reasonable claim when we consider that individuals tend to be more refreshed and productive at certain hours of the day. Some people in the arts are more creative in the early morning hours. Others feel that their minds are more receptive to creative ideas late at night. And too, there may be fewer environmental disturbances during certain parts of the day. For example, in the residential areas of town, traffic is heavier during the rush hours of early morning and evening. Children are away at school during the winter days, and, in the case of small children, they go to bed early at night.

Some readers even claim that no reading should be attempted on a day that is foggy, windy, rainy, or stormy. Again, this may not be so far-fetched as it at first sounds. Such adverse atmospheric conditions not only would tend to produce static conditions that would interfere with the vibrations involved in a reading, but also would present distractions to the deep concentration necessary for a reading. How can you keep your mind on the business at hand with thunder and lightning outside your windows?

Probably all the aforementioned claims hold some truth, but they are based upon individual findings. The best time for one person to read the Tarot cards may not be the best time for another. You may have to experiment with various days and hours, under varying atmospheric conditions, and keep a record of the known successes and failures of your readings to determine if there is a best time for you to undertake your readings.

WHERE TO SPREAD THE CARDS

The next thing to consider is the surface on which you spread the cards. Based on the principles of radiation, it is best to have a special Tarot board made of unfinished white pine. Since this soft wood is a poor conductor of vibrations, the chance of present readings being disturbed by vibrations of bygone sessions is minimized.

Preliminary to the Divinatory Reading

A Tarot board should be large enough to spread sixteen cards across its breadth, with a little space between each card. And it should hold nine cards interspaced from the top to the bottom. With a Tarot deck of standard size, this calls for a table or board of at least four and a half feet by five feet. This should accommodate the largest of the Tarot spreads.

WHERE TO READ THE CARDS

The next consideration is where to conduct the reading, for environment has an important bearing on the results of the session. Have you ever entered a house where you "felt" the domestic condition of its occupants? In some houses the lamps, chairs, curtains, walls, and so on seem to produce cold, discordant feelings, while the contents of many other homes produce warm, pleasant feelings. Many people have experienced this vibratory sensation. Once you understand the basic principles of radiation you will appreciate how environment can affect the Tarot reading. When the environmental vibrations are peaceful and harmonious the reading progresses smoothly; but when a particular environment reflects an air of violence, quarreling, or other discordant vibratory "ghosts" of the past, static conditions invariably interfere with the reading.

THE MEANING OF TAROT
WHO SHOULD BE PRESENT?

In the ideal situation, no one but the reader and the inquirer are present in the room during a Tarot reading. This eliminates the interplay of vibrations from persons involved directly in the reading. When the reader and the inquirer concentrate their undivided attention upon the essentials of the reading, psychic emanations, which are picked up by the natural attraction of the Tarot cards, flow freely between the two participants. Then a sort of "vibratory computer" system takes over, causing certain cards to fall into a special place in the spread.

WHERE TO SIT

The inquirer and the reader should sit opposite the board from each other in a north-to-south direction. Since the flow of the earth's natural magnetic current is from north to south, the inquirer should sit with his back to the north and facing the reader whose back is toward the south. Then the vibrations of the inquirer at the north or positive end of the board will flow toward the reader at the south or negative end. When these positive and negative elements meet, a current of energy is released to the Tarot cards. This vibratory message determines which cards form the spread and their relative position.

Preliminary to the Divinatory Reading

READING FOR YOURSELF OR FOR ABSENT INQUIRERS

There may be times when you are called upon to give a reading for an inquirer who cannot be present during the reading. This can be done if you concentrate hard upon the inquirer, for there is no time or distance barrier to a properly tuned vibratory channel. Nevertheless, the reading is easier when the inquirer sends you some personal item to touch. When reading the cards for an absent inquirer, or for yourself, sit at the board facing east. Then, in privacy, shuffle, cut, and spread the cards to proceed with the reading.

NATURE OF THE PRELIMINARY CONVERSATION

Few inquirers have any knowledge of the Tarot other than knowing it is an instrument of divination. Before the Tarot cards are removed from their box and purple cloth, therefore, the reader should seek to establish a rapport with the inquirer by briefly discussing what the Tarot is and the general principles of how it works. If the inquirer appears uneasy after this preliminary "warm-up," it may be desirable to mention the importance of the Tarot symbols *without revealing their divinatory meanings.* Reflection upon the higher nature of these symbols

THE MEANING OF TAROT

is often reassuring to a troubled inquirer. But if the inquirer shows any indication of scorn or doubt it may be well to cancel the reading. The success of the reading depends a good deal upon establishing a rapport between inquirer and reader, whereby the cards form a bridge linking their subconscious minds. Thus, the vibrations of the inquirer are sensitized to the reader's wave length and communicate to the reader subconscious thoughts, emotional responses, and subtle reactions.

When the inquirer approaches the Tarot with an objective attitude and rapport has been established, the conversation should be directed toward the goals to be accomplished in the reading. Any distraction or small talk tends to hinder the law of natural vibratory attraction. The reader should instruct the inquirer to be serious throughout the reading and to concentrate upon what he wishes to accomplish, so that vibrations bearing only on the reading will permeate the atmosphere.

PINPOINTING THE INQUIRY

The reader should ask the inquirer to specify what information he desires from the cards. It is important to ask a definite question. But since questions are sometimes asked incorrectly, the reader should pinpoint the actual inquiry by discussing the background leading to the inquirer's reason for the consultation. Clearly defining the

Preliminary to the Divinatory Reading

question focuses the attention of the subconscious on the specific information desired, and it helps the reader to select the appropriate spread and the suitable divinatory meaning of each card. Since each card has one distinct meaning with several parts, the reader must choose the part that best relates to the question and to the other cards in the spread.

SELECTING THE SPREAD

The spread is an orderly and established arrangement of cards on the Tarot board. A specified number of cards is used in each layout. The cards in the spread stand for people, things, places, or events. Although each card has a meaning all its own, it is influenced by the total spread and especially by the cards adjacent to it. Each spread has an established route to be followed while interpreting the cards. Many varieties of spreads are used by Tarot readers. Some of the spreads are quite intricate and many of them are associated with astrology, numerology, the Cabala, or other occult sciences.

Generally, the various spreads answer questions that come under three comprehensive classifications: personal questions; general questions of local or universal concern; and religious, spiritual, or philosophical questions. Furthermore, the questions can be broken down into subclassifications as follows: those requiring simple

THE MEANING OF TAROT

answers; those requiring complex answers; those involved with the present time or near future; and those involving periods of time extending far into the future.

Some of the spreads are specialized to answer the questions in a particular classification better. For example, the Yes or No Spread serves those questions that can be answered with a simple "yes or no." The Three Sevens Spread is designed to give quick answers to problems that are not too complicated. More complex problems might better be answered by such encompassing spreads as the Individual Horoscope Spread or the Spread of 36. Either the Tree of Life Spread or the Ancient Celtic Spread may be used to determine the outcome of any question dealing with the near future. Questions involving periods of time extending farther into the future might best be answered with the Victory Cross Spread or the Pyramid Spread.

The type of spread to be used in a reading is chosen by the reader as he listens to the inquirer relate the circumstances that led him to the Tarot board in search of answers. From these facts, the reader pinpoints the information desired of the cards and determines which spread would give that information best.

SHUFFLING AND CUTTING

Before touching the cards, the reader must cleanse his thoughts of all pettiness, malice, greed, selfishness, and

Preliminary to the Divinatory Reading

desire for material gain or vindication. He must dedicate himself to the service of the inquirer. Similarly, the inquirer should be cautioned that if he plans to use the information of the reading for unworthy intentions, the cards, while revealing the outcome of his inquiry, may give the wrong guidance or instruction as to how the outcome will be achieved. He should concentrate on the idea that the true answer to his question will be revealed regardless of what he would like the answer to be.

One further caution is advisable concerning the intentions of the inquirer at the reading. It is unlikely that an inquirer will return for a second reading with the same, or slightly modified inquiry, just to test the consistency of the answers of the two readings. But if this should happen, the answer given by the cards will not apply to the specific question asked. The Tarot does not lend itself to petty examination.

Throughout the entire process of shuffling and cutting, the inquirer must maintain this attitude of concentration, while the reader makes his mind as passive as possible. Thus, the direction of thought is controlled and soon results in the necessary intramuscular activity.

Then the reader hands the entire deck of seventy-eight cards to the inquirer and asks him to place his hands on them while thinking attentively on the objectives just mentioned. With this completed, the reader takes the deck and spreads the cards face down on the board. Then he turns some of the cards upside down so that they are in what is known as a reversed position. The reader may reverse however many cards he feels impressed to do. *His intuition leads the way.* These cards have a slightly different meaning, which will be discussed later. (After

THE MEANING OF TAROT

every reading the cards are restored to their upright position, ready for future use.)

At this point, the reader gathers the cards and shuffles them slowly, using the overhand method, until he feels impressed to stop. He should never break or riffle the cards. Remember that during the shuffle, the reader's conscious mind remains passive so that his subconscious mind can direct the operation.

Since the deck of seventy-eight cards is larger than a deck of ordinary playing cards, it is a little more difficult to handle at first. Turning the cards lengthwise makes the shuffle easier. (The same method of shuffling should be used at every reading.) When the mechanics of the shuffle becomes a habit, it no longer poses a distraction to the accompanying concentration.

After the cards have been thoroughly shuffled, the reader hands the deck to the inquirer who places it to his own immediate left on the board. Then, starting at this position and moving toward the right, he cuts the deck into three separate stacks using his left hand, the hand nearest the heart. When this has been completed the inquirer places the left stack on top of the middle one and then places this combined stack on top of the stack to the right and hands the whole deck back to the reader. This procedure of shuffling and cutting the cards is performed a total of three times. This ritual helps to produce an interaction of the subconscious minds of the participants. But, after the shuffling and cutting has been completed, the inquirer does not touch the cards again during the session.

Preliminary to the Divinatory Reading
SPREADING THE CARDS

Now that the spread has been decided and the shuffling and cutting has been completed, the reader is ready to deal the cards into the pattern of the chosen spread. The cards are dealt from right to left with the faces down until the pattern is completed. This pattern should be constructed to be viewed from where the reader sits. The reader then places the cards not used back into the Tarot box. (Whenever the arrangement of a spread makes it impossible to deal from right to left or in a clockwise direction, the cards should be dealt in the order in which they will be explained in the reading.)

The *theory* behind the right-to-left direction of dealing is that the right hand is positive and the left hand is negative and since the positive is attracted to the negative, a right-to-left movement facilitates a meeting of the two charges which in turn causes a flow of magnetic current. This current is a sort of messenger that carries the "news" of the cards to the subconscious.

READING THE CARDS

When the reader is ready to begin the divination, he lifts the top of one card at a time and pulls it over toward himself, exposing the face of the card so that he can detect

THE MEANING OF TAROT

its significance before progressing to the next card in the sequence. This keeps his mind from wandering to the other cards at random, which would disturb the thought pattern.

But since the position of the cards in the spread also has a bearing on the reading, and because certain cards appearing together in a spread mean something, the reader should never comment on individual cards until he has an impression of the full story. Once he has the feel of the entire story, the reader can make a smoothly flowing story from the information he read in the cards. His intuition helps him to link together the divinatory meanings of the separate cards.

During the process of piecing the thoughts together, however, the reader should never try to guess or alter the meanings of the cards themselves, but should adhere strictly to the traditional meanings. The use of logic to analyze the cards into the inquirer's background would interfere with the impressions of the subconscious. There are special cases, however, when meanings may be modified, expanded, or partially omitted. For instance, it is not advisable to predict morbid conditions or events, such as the inquirer's death, even though the cards indicate such an occurrence.

It should be pointed out that the Tarot is not based on fatalism. The cards usually indicate only general trends, traits, and influences which, if not consciously altered, will lead to a predictable conclusion. Thus, the Tarot is a valuable tool in uncovering the course of events that needs to be changed or circumvented.

Cards appearing in reversed, that is, upside down, positions usually convey a less favorable or potent mean-

Preliminary to the Divinatory Reading

ing. The reader should be well versed in both the upright and the reversed meanings.

UNSATISFACTORY READINGS

The interpretation of the spread depends upon the reader's mastery of the divinatory meanings. If he has thoroughly learned all seventy-eight cards, he should be able to give a most satisfactory reading.

Nevertheless, if the inquirer feels that the reader did not give him an adequate answer to his question, he should be asked to restate his original question and then compare it with the question he asked at the start of the session. The reader may find that the original question was superficial and that the inquirer left out some pertinent information in his background story. The reader then should ask if he answered some other question the inquirer had in his mind or if, perhaps, an answer has been given to a deeper problem that was not consciously on the inquirer's mind at the time. The Tarot often gets to a root cause, buried in the subconscious, of many of the smaller problems at the surface.

If the inquirer still thinks that the reader has not answered his specific question, it is advisable not to attempt the reading again that day, but to reschedule it for a later date. In the meantime, the inquirer may find that the reader uncovered a deeper problem after all.

Part Four

Methods of Divination

WE NOW come to the practical division of our subject, the art of Tarot divination. To carry out the instructions in this chapter, you will need a complete Tarot pack of seventy-eight cards. It is also imperative that you learn the divinatory meanings of all seventy-eight cards before you attempt to give a reading. The known Tarot spreads and methods of divination are rather numerous, and some of them are quite complicated. Therefore, it is advisable to start with the easier methods, in the order given in this chapter. After you feel comfortable with these methods, you may then proceed to the more complicated ones. You will notice that some of the Tarot spreads are intended for predicting the future in general, while others are applicable to seeking solutions to specific questions.

Some spreads call for a Significator; that is, a card to represent the person about which inquiry is made. In these cases the reader selects a Court card from the deck which corresponds to that person's personal description. This is done before the cards are shuffled and laid out in a spread. The inquirer is usually the main character of the inquiry,

THE MEANING OF TAROT

or the reader may wish to consult the cards for his own personal reading.

In any event, if the person of inquiry is an adult male, a King should be chosen from the suit that matches his personal description. A Horseman may also be used if his physical characteristics match those of the person of inquiry. A Queen from the appropriate suit should be chosen for an adult female. And an Attendant may be used for children of either sex. When a Court card is used as a Significator, its divinatory meaning is not incorporated into the reading.

In the Court cards, each King differs in physical characteristics and temperament. The same is true of the Queens, Horsemen, and Attendants, respectively. The Wands represent individuals with very fair complexions, blond or auburn hair, and blue eyes. The Cups represent people having rather fair complexions, light brown or dull, fair hair, and gray, blue, or hazel eyes. The Swords represent people with darker complexions, dark brown hair, and brown, hazel, or gray eyes. The Pentacles represent individuals with sallow or swarthy complexions, very dark brown or black hair, and dark eyes.

If you have thoroughly studied the divinatory meanings and feel well enough acquainted with them, you are now ready to attempt the fascinating art of divination. If no one volunteers to be an inquirer, it is best not to try to persuade him. A person must come to the cards with a legitimate purpose—to honestly seek an answer to a problem. You can gain much practice on yourself and gradually develop the skills necessary to be a master Tarot reader. The instructions throughout this chapter are addressed to "you," as the divinatory reader.

Methods of Divination
PYRAMID SPREAD

This is a good spread for detailed analysis of a problem as well as for answering a question or indicating the trend of events of a person's near or distant future.

After the cards have been shuffled and cut, deal twenty cards face downward, from right to left, starting with the bottom row of the pyramid. Seven cards are placed along the bottom row, six on the second row, four on the third row, two on the next row, and one card at the top.

Starting at the right on the bottom row and working to the left and upward, the first five cards represent the past, and the next four cards represent the present. The next four cards represent the immediate future, and the four after that indicate the next trend of events. The last four cards give the outcome of the subject of inquiry.

PYRAMID SPREAD

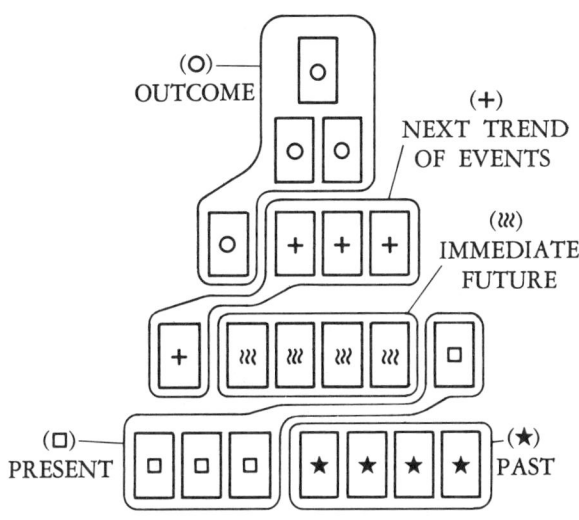

THE MEANING OF TAROT

THREE SEVENS SPREAD

This spread may be used to obtain short, simple answers giving the past, present, and future aspects of the circumstances involved in the subject of inquiry.

Withdraw from the pack the Court card selected as the inquirer's Significator. Then shuffle and cut in the usual manner. Place the Significator on the board face up.

Now hold the deck of cards so the faces are down. Then go through the pack starting with the card on top and select every seventh card to be placed on the board as indicated in the diagram. When you have dealt twenty-one cards, stop and place the other cards aside, face down in a stack.

Future
Present
Past

The bottom row represents the conditions or events of the past leading to the present situation, which is represented by the middle row. And the top row indicates the future of the subject of inquiry. Read the cards in each row from right to left, beginning with the Significator which must be moved into place alongside each row as needed.

For further information on the subject, combine the cards into pairs as follows:

Cards 1 and 21   Cards 5 and 17
Cards 2 and 20   Cards 6 and 16
Cards 3 and 19   Cards 7 and 15
Cards 4 and 18

Methods of Divination

Then read the combined meanings of all the pairs so as to make a connected answer. Whether this additional information deals with the past, the present, or the future depends upon the nature of the combined pairs.

THREE SEVENS SPREAD

FUTURE |21| |20| |19| |18| |17| |16| |15|

PRESENT |14| |13| |12| |11| |10| |9| |8|

PAST |7| |6| |5| |4| |3| |2| |1|

                                    | |
                              SIGNIFICATOR

THE MEANING OF TAROT

SPREAD OF 35

Although this spread is a separate entity, it may also be used after the Three Sevens Spread to explain further or to clarify anything about the earlier answer that remains doubtful. Even when the answer of the previous reading was clearly stated, this spread may be used to explore deeper into the subject.

When this spread supplements the Three Sevens Spread, use only the thirty-five cards that were *not* dealt in the previous reading. Set the other cards aside in a stack, with the Significator on top.

Thirty-five cards should be shuffled and cut as before and dealt face down into six horizontal stacks from right to left, as in the diagram.

SPREAD OF 35

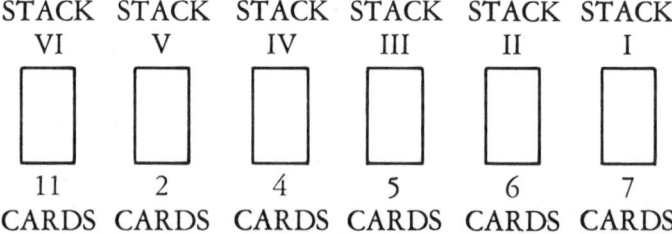

The first stack should have seven cards; the second, six cards, the third, five cards; the fourth, four cards; the fifth, two cards; and the sixth, eleven cards.

Now, take each stack separately and spread its cards face up in a vertical line, starting at the top and working downward. Then, starting at the top right card, read the cards in

Methods of Divination

each line, from top to bottom, progressing from right to left.

The cards in the first line at the extreme right give a reading pertaining to the inquirer's home, his position in life, the influence of immediate friends, and any other tendencies at work in his environment.

The cards in the second line together tell the position or attitude of the person or subject of inquiry in the circumstances.

The third line reveals the influences, events, or persons outside the environment of the person or subject of inquiry which will have a bearing on the outcome of the situation in question.

The fourth line reveals any unexpected events, arrivals, persons, or surprises of any kind in connection with the situation in question.

The fifth line foresees any circumstances that may be a consolation, and thus, through this foreknowledge, may somewhat moderate the effects of any unfavorable predictions in the preceding lines.

The sixth line's only importance is to explain further or clarify any perplexing or mysterious pronouncements of the other lines.

THE MEANING OF TAROT
SPREAD OF 36

This spread is used to give answers to questions involving detailed answers. After the cards have been shuffled and cut in the routine manner, you deal thirty-six cards face down, from right to left, as shown in the diagram.

Read the bottom row, from right to left, to get a reading of the past circumstances that led up to the present situation of the subject of inquiry. Next, read the second row, from right to left, to explain the present situation further. Then, start with Card 13 and progress from right to left until you have read the remaining cards in the spread in numerical order. This should give a detailed picture of the future situation of the subject of inquiry. If the inquirer desires further information concerning the question or feels something remains doubtful in the answer, you may gather more divinatory information by pairing the cards in the following manner:

Cards 1 and 36	Cards 7 and 30	Cards 13 and 24
Cards 2 and 35	Cards 8 and 29	Cards 14 and 23
Cards 3 and 34	Cards 9 and 28	Cards 15 and 22
Cards 4 and 33	Cards 10 and 27	Cards 16 and 21
Cards 5 and 32	Cards 11 and 26	Cards 17 and 20
Cards 6 and 31	Cards 12 and 25	Cards 18 and 19

These pairings will add details to the reading of the original Spread of 36. Whether the additional information deals with the past, the present, or the future depends upon the nature of each pair of cards. Whereas one pair may deal with the future, another pair may concern itself with the past.

Methods of Divination

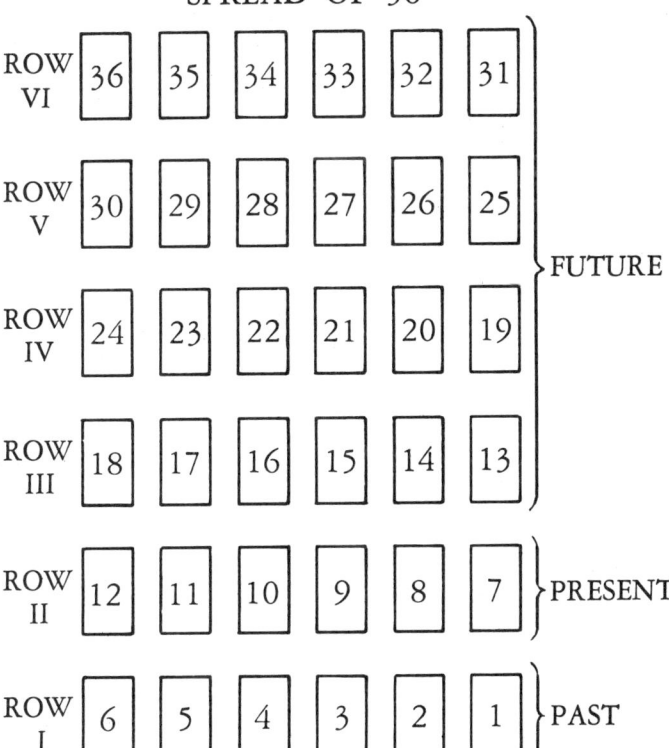

THE MEANING OF TAROT
HORSESHOE SPREAD

This is a very ancient and reliable method of reading the Tarot. It is complex and may be used for either a general reading or to answer a specific question involving a detailed answer. In this operation the reader deals out the entire deck into two stacks designated as A and B. Start by placing the top card down for the start of Stack B and then lay the next top card down for Stack A. After the initial card has been placed on the table for each stack, continue drawing from the top and place *two* cards on Stack B for every *one* you place on Stack A.

After this has been completed, put Stack B aside. It will not be used.

At this point you should be extra careful to keep the Stack A cards in the order in which they are arranged. One misplaced card could alter the reading drastically. Now you are ready to arrange the twenty-six cards of Stack A in the form of a horseshoe with the ends pointing toward yourself. As you begin, place the top card of Stack A to your right with the face up. Continue to build the horseshoe from right to left, using the top cards face up. When you are finished, the twenty-sixth card will be at the left end of the horseshoe.

Working from right to left, read the divinatory meanings of the cards so as to make a connected answer of general reading. When this has been determined, start with the first and twenty-sixth cards and pair each card with the one straight across from it on the horseshoe. (The last pair will be the thirteenth and fourteenth cards.) Now read the combined meanings of each pair.

Methods of Divination

THE HORSESHOE SPREAD

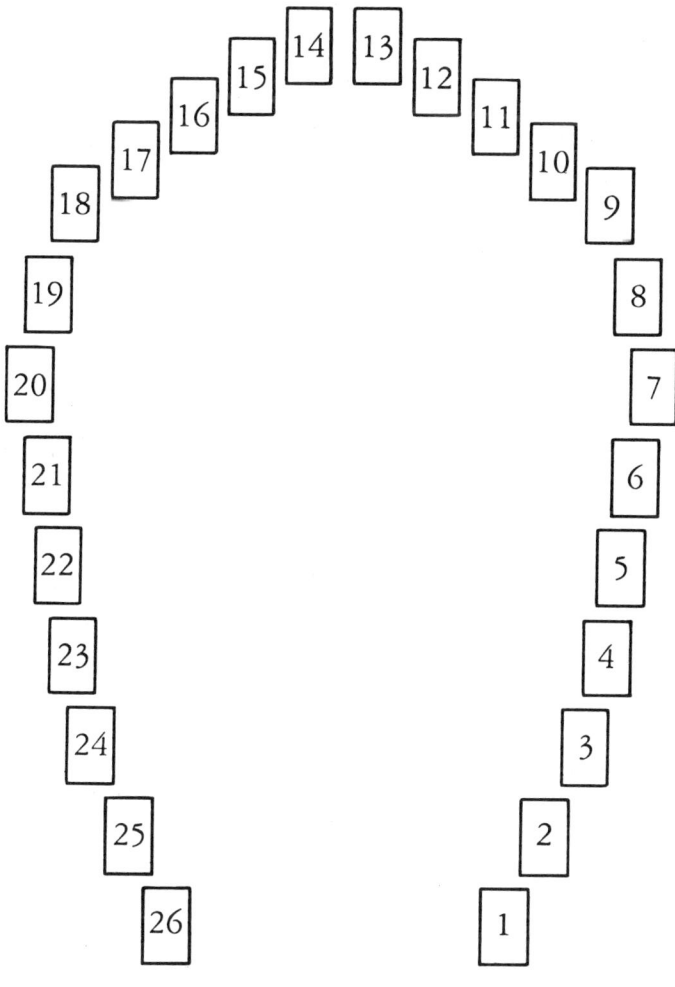

THE MEANING OF TAROT
PERSONAL HOROSCOPE SPREAD

This spread is usually used to give a general life reading. Select the appropriate card to be the Significator, and place it face up in the center of the board as a control card for this spread. Then, after shuffling and cutting the cards in the usual manner, deal the top twelve cards into a wide circle around the Significator. Starting with Card 1 at the top of the circle, the cards should be dealt face down in a clockwise sequence. These twelve cards represent the twelve Houses of a horoscope, as in astrology. Therefore, you should correlate the interpretation of each card with the general quality of the respective House in which it is located. Turn the cards over one at a time to read them, starting with Card 1 at the top of the circle.

The general meanings of the Solar Houses are:

Solar House	*Activities or People Represented*
Card 1	Represents the inquirer's Solar House. It should be understood that he may not have been born under the sign of the House in which this card is located. Its position just tells you that the inquirer has the traits of this House.
Card 2	Money, finances, and movable possessions. Gain or loss, according to the card's prediction.

Methods of Divination

Solar House	Activities or People Represented
Card 3	Brothers and sisters; mental outlook, inclinations, and abilities; short journeys; changes; writings, letters, and telephone calls.
Card 4	Father; home, property and immovable possessions (real estate); environment; domestic affairs; and lands.
Card 5	Children; particularly his first child; love affairs; sport, pleasure and speculation.
Card 6	Health; service conditions; food, clothing, hygiene; small animals.
Card 7	Marriage; courtships, unions, partnerships, contracts, general relations or dealings with other people; legal affairs; open animosities.
Card 8	Death; psychic experiences of a spiritual nature; all matters arising from a death, such as wills, settlements, arrangements, adjustments, etc.; also insurances, taxation, money belonging to others, financial affairs of the spouse or business partner.

THE MEANING OF TAROT

Solar House	Activities or People Represented
Card 9	Future arrangements; long journeys, foreign countries, places far removed from birthplace; relaxations; legal questions; religion; philosophy; education; visions; dreams; psychic development.
Card 10	Mother; profession, occupation, career, and status; employer; relationships with authorities; promotion; ambitions; fame; honor. Also affairs of government.
Card 11	Friends, associations, clubs and societies; hopes, wishes, fears, bodily comforts.
Card 12	Unexpected or unseen troubles; hidden or secret enemies, hatreds; the results of past activities. Restraint, limitations, prisons, hospitals, mental institutions, sanitariums. Anything withheld or concealed in the inquirer's mind concerning the reading. Large animals. Secret societies and organizations devoted to practical occultism.

Methods of Divination

PERSONAL HOROSCOPE SPREAD

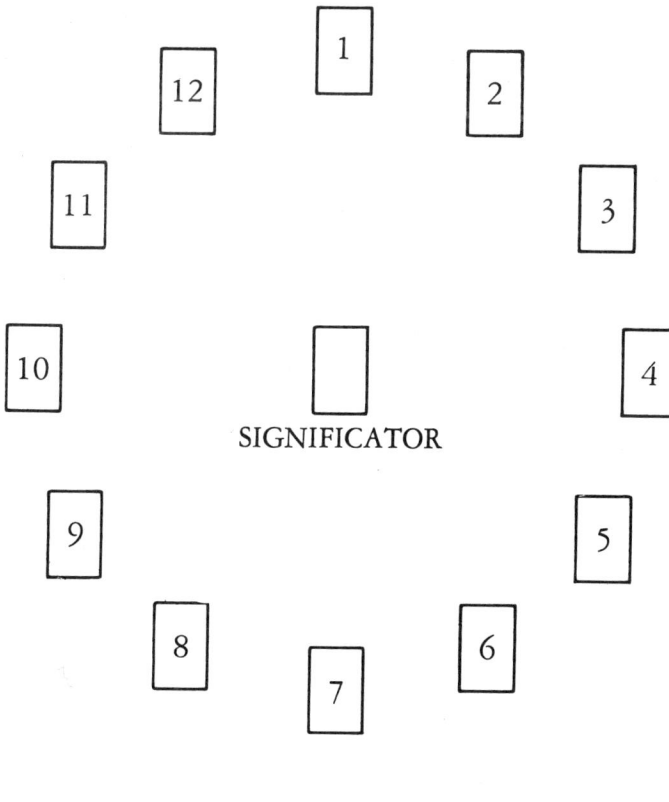

THE MEANING OF TAROT

YES OR NO SPREAD

The purpose of this spread is to give a quick yes or no answer to a question. For short uncomplicated questions, use five cards. For long, detailed questions that can be given a yes or no answer, use nine cards. For questions between these extremes, use seven cards. Remember that the questions must be asked in a manner that can be answered yes or no. If they are framed otherwise, the answer will be indefinite.

A. Simple Yes or No Spread

After shuffling and cutting the seventy-eight cards in the usual manner, deal the top card face down on the board to your right. Then deal the next four cards one at a time and place them face down to the left of the first card, as in the diagram.

SIMPLE YES OR NO SPREAD

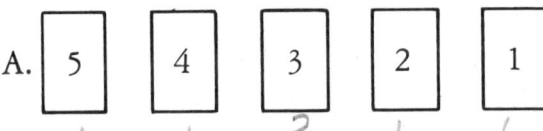

The value of the card in the center of the spread (Card 3) is two. The other cards each have a value of one. Each card retains the same respective value regardless of an upright or reversed position. To get an answer to the question, total the values of the upright cards. Then total the values of the reversed cards. If the upright cards have a larger total value, the answer is yes; but if the reversed cards have a larger total, the answer is no. In the event the upright and the reversed cards should have the same total value, the answer is indefinite. This would indicate

Methods of Divination

that the inquirer did not concentrate strongly enough, with a desire for a true answer.

B. Detailed Yes or No Spread

When an inquirer desires a more detailed yes or no answer, follow the same procedure as in the Simple Yes or No Spread. After the answer to the question has been determined, additional information may be obtained with the special features of the Detailed Yes or No Spread. Cards 1 and 2 will tell the past conditions and events that led to the present situation of the subject of inquiry. The middle card explains the present situation of the subject. And Cards 4 and 5 reveal the nature of the circumstances surrounding the subject in the future. It does not reveal the outcome, however, unless that was the specific question asked.

DETAILED YES OR NO SPREAD

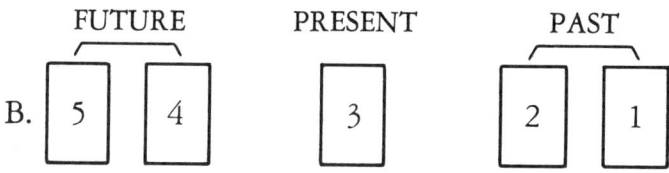

If the answer to the question was affirmative, read the divinatory meanings of each card in sequence, starting with those of the past and working toward the cards of the future. This reading will tell why the answer was affirmative, or how the affirmative situation will come about.

If the answer to the question was negative, follow the same reading instructions as in the case of the affirmative. This reading will tell the inquirer how to "live with" the situation.

THE MEANING OF TAROT
TREE OF LIFE SPREAD

This spread may be used to give a general life reading and indicates the spiritual, intellectual, and material trends in the inquirer's life. This spread involves the near future.

Select the appropriate card to be the Significator, and place it face down high in the center of the board. Then shuffle and cut the cards in the usual manner, and lay out the first nine cards face down in three triangles below the Significator. Now place a tenth card beneath the triangles. (See diagram.) This pattern forms the Tree of Life.

Place the next seven cards from the deck face down in a stack at the extreme left of the tenth card. This reserve deck is call the *Death*, or qualifying pack.

Now turn over each card in sequence and read it, starting with Card 1.

Triangle 1 points upward and is formed by Cards 1, 2, and 3. Card 1 is at the apex, while Cards 2 and 3 are at each corner of the base. This triangle represents the spiritual trend, the highest ideal in the inquirer's life.

Triangle 2 points downward and is formed by Cards 4, 5, and 6. Card 6 is at the lowest point of the triangle, while Cards 4 and 5 are at each corner of the base. This triangle represents the intellectual and moral trend in the life of the inquirer.

Triangle 3 also points downward and is formed by Cards 7, 8, and 9. Card 9 is at the lowest point, while Cards 7 and 8 are at each corner of the base. This triangle represents the material trend, the intuitions, desires, and impulses in the subconsciousness of the inquirer.

Card 1 represents the inquirer's highest intelligence and

Methods of Divination
TREE OF LIFE SPREAD

SIGNIFICATOR

1
3 2

SPIRITUAL NATURE

5 4
6

8 7
9

INTELLECTUAL &
MORAL NATURE

INTUITIONAL &
DESIRE NATURE

10
BRANCH OF
HARMONY

DEATH PACK

thus indicates the potential mental forces he has to use in meeting the challenges of life.

Card 2 is the "father" card and represents the inquirer's creative force as a potential parent. It indicates the number of children he will have.

THE MEANING OF TAROT

Card 3 is the "mother" card and represents the nature of the inquirer's life and his wisdom. The kind of life he lives and the degree of wisdom he uses in his circumstances gives an indication of his ability to meet the challenge of life.

Card 4 represents the inquirer's virtues and good qualities, which may be a help in his everyday life if they are used to advantage.

Card 5 represents the inquirer's conquering initiative and his intellectual or physical forces. It indicates his drive, or lack of it, in conquering or overcoming obstacles. It also indicates his desire and drive to succeed.

Card 6 represents the inquirer's present health and his spirit of sacrifice. It indicates his ability to stand up under the pressures of life and his willingness to surrender pleasure and other activities to devote his time toward his goals. It predicts the condition of his health in the future.

Card 7 is the Venus card and represents the inquirer's love and lust. It indicates his personal attachments and his marital faithfulness, or lack of it.

Card 8 represents the inquirer's art and craft abilities. This card may uncover hidden talents.

Card 9 represents the inquirer's imagination and his creative mental and physical forces. It indicates his ability to find exciting but worthwhile new experiences in life. It also indicates his ability to find new directions in life, or new approaches to situations in life.

Card 10 represents the inquirer's physical body or his home in this life. It indicates the condition of the environment in which he spends his life. It may also indicate his life span.

Now that you have finished reading the cards on the

Methods of Divination

Tree of Life, turn up the top card in the Death pack and place it at the bottom of the board. Then place each succeeding top card to the left of the first one. The reading should also be from the right to the left. These seven cards represent conditions, events, and situations that are developing at the present, but will come to a head in the immediate future.

The arrangement of the cards in this spread forms three branches on the Tree of Life. The cards on the left branch, or Branch of Discipline, should be given a strict, unbending interpretation. The cards on the middle branch, or Branch of Harmony, should be allowed a lenient interpretation. And those on the right branch, or Branch of Love, should be read in a spirit of love and compassion.

THE MEANING OF TAROT
ANCIENT CELTIC SPREAD

This spread may be used to give general life readings or to answer specific questions involving detailed answers. It involves the near future. Ten cards are used in this spread. Before the cards are dealt, one of the Court cards is chosen to be the Significator and placed on the board, face up. It does not matter if the Significator is upright or reversed, for the spread is always read from the reader's position at the board. After reversing any of the remaining seventy-seven cards, the reader shuffles them and places the deck to the left of the inquirer. Using the left hand, the inquirer cuts the deck into three stacks, moving from left to right. Then starting with the left stack, he regathers the cards into one deck, keeping the cards face down, and hands it back to the reader, who proceeds as follows:

Turn up the top card and lay it directly on top of the Significator, saying, "This covers you."

Turn up the next card in the deck and lay it on the board across the first card, saying, "This crosses you."

Turn up the third card and place it on the board below the Significator, saying, "This is beneath you."

Turn up the fourth card and place it to the left of the Significator, saying, "This is behind you."

Turn up the fifth card and place it above the Significator, saying, "This is above you."

Turn up the sixth card and place it to the immediate right of the Significator, saying, "This is in front of you."

These six cards now form a cross, with the Significator at the very center.

Now turn up the next four cards in the deck, one at a

Methods of Divination

time, and place them one above the other in a vertical column to the right of the cross. The seventh card will be on the bottom of the column and the tenth card will be at the top.

If several Court cards should happen to appear in a spread, whether of the same suit or not, they may convey special messages according to the suit in which they belong. Court cards in the Cups suit may indicate happy company; Wands may indicate a business consultation or convention; Swords may indicate conflict; and Pentacles may indicate politics. Two Kings appearing in a spread may indicate a consultation or conference; two Queens face to face may indicate gossip; two Horsemen may indicate conflict; and two Attendants may indicate "sportive recreation."

Card 1. This is what covers the inquirer. It reveals both the most important influences affecting and the general atmosphere surrounding the inquirer's present situation, or the subject of his inquiry.

Card 2. This is what crosses the inquirer. Even though this card lies on its side, it is read as an upright card, rather than a reversed card. It indicates the opposing forces in the subject of inquiry. If the card is otherwise a favorable card, the obstacles will not be of grave nature.

Card 3. This is what is beneath the inquirer. It reveals whatever it was in the inquirer's past experience that became the basis or foundation of the subject of his inquiry. Thus it may also reveal the

THE MEANING OF TAROT

strongest basic influence on him in this particular matter.

Card 4. This is what is behind the inquirer. It gives an influence that has just passed or is now waning.

Card 5. This is what is above the inquirer. It represents the inquirer's goal or the best he can achieve in this matter, considering the circumstances.

Card 6. This is what is in front of the inquirer. It indicates an influence that is developing and will soon be in operation.

Card 7. This is the inquirer. It shows his position or attitude in the subject of inquiry and reveals any strength or weakness in his makeup that may have a bearing on the outcome.

Card 8. This is the inquirer's house or environment. It represents the opinions of his family, friends, and associates and the influences and tendencies of his environment that have an effect on the subject of his inquiry.

Card 9. These are the inquirer's hopes and fears. It reveals how he wishes to obtain his goal and what misgivings or even intimidations he may have as he strives toward his goal or solution to his problem.

Card 10. This is the inquirer's future. It tells the probable outcome of all that was revealed in the other cards of the spread.

Methods of Divination
ANCIENT CELTIC SPREAD

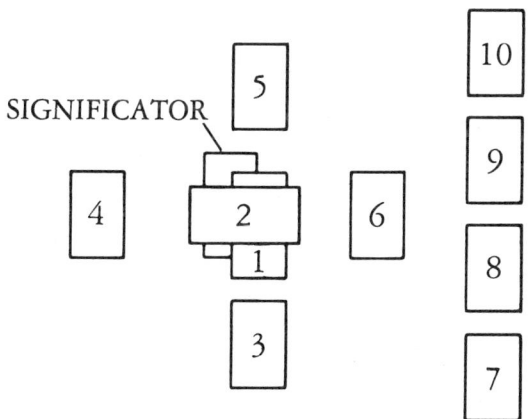

The Significator is completely covered by the first card.

1. This is what covers him.
2. This is what crosses him.
3. This is what is beneath him.
4. This is what is behind him.
5. This is what is above him.
6. This is what is in front of him.
7. This is the inquirer.
8. This is his house.
9. These are his hopes and fears.
10. This is his future.

THE MEANING OF TAROT

VICTORY CROSS SPREAD

This spread may be used to answer questions involving the distant future. After the cards have been shuffled and cut in the usual manner, deal the top thirteen cards out in the form of a cross. (See diagram.)

Cards 1 and 2 uncover the past circumstances that led to the present situation of the subject of inquiry. Card 3 tells the true nature of the situation at the present. Cards 4 and 5 reveal what forces are in opposition to the subject of inquiry. Cards 6 and 7 reveal the hopes and expectations of the inquirer or the person for whom the inquiry is made. And Cards 8 through 13 tell the future outcome of the subject of inquiry.

VICTORY CROSS SPREAD

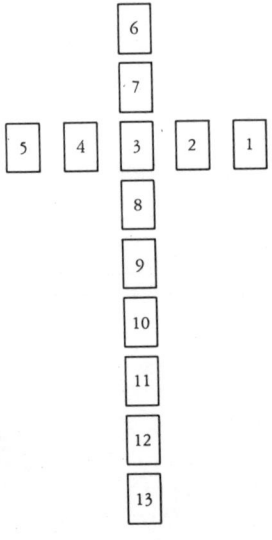

Part Five

The Major Arcana

THE more important division of the Tarot, called the Major Arcana or Greater Arcana, consists of twenty-two cards numbered consecutively from I through XXII. The appropriate number is given as a Roman numeral at the top of each card. These numbers stand for the sequence of the cards, but not for the numerical values of the corresponding Hebrew letters at the bottom of each card.

Although the Roman numerals designating the order of the Major Arcana cards are in numerical sequence from I through XXII, the letter-values of the corresponding Hebrew alphabet are not arranged in such a continuous series. In the first nine cards, using the Hebrew letters aleph to teth, the corresponding numerical values are given in digits, from 1 to 9 consecutively. In the next nine cards, from the letters yod to tsadi, the corresponding numbers are given in tens, from 10 to 90. And in the last four cards, using the letters koph to tav, the numerical values are given in hundreds, from 100 to 400. This arrangement of Hebrew letters and numerical values differs with various Tarot writers, however.

THE MEANING OF TAROT

There has been much discussion and some disagreement among Tarot scholars as to the proper sequence of the twenty-two cards. Some writers place the Fool at the end of the Major Arcana, and assign it the Hebrew letter tav and the numerical value of either zero or 400. Still others place it as it is in this book, before the last card in the Major Arcana, and assign it the Hebrew letter shin and the numerical value 300.

There have also been variations in the placement of the cards known as Strength and Justice. Although in this book the number XI is assigned to Strength and VIII is assigned to Justice, some writers reverse this arrangement. Nonetheless, the first arrangement is in accordance with an old tradition, and was used in esoteric editions of the Tarot in France and Italy after the eighteenth century.

Each card of the Major Arcana contains a picture of some character representing an esoteric truth. The title of each card lends a clue to its meaning. But even this can be deceptive, as the name Temperance on Arcanum XIV does not denote the usual meaning of the word at all.

The twenty-two illustrations on the Major Arcana cards, as also with the fifty-six cards of the Minor Arcana, were designed from traditional occult interpretations that were originally confined within the brotherhood of secret organizations.

THE MAJOR ARCANA

III. The Empress

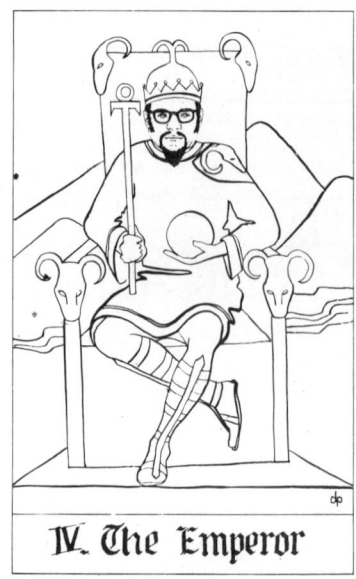

IV. The Emperor

V. The Hierophant

VI. The Lovers

VII. The Chariot

VIII. Justice

IX. The Hermit

X. The Wheel of Fortune

XI. Strength

XII. The Hanged Man

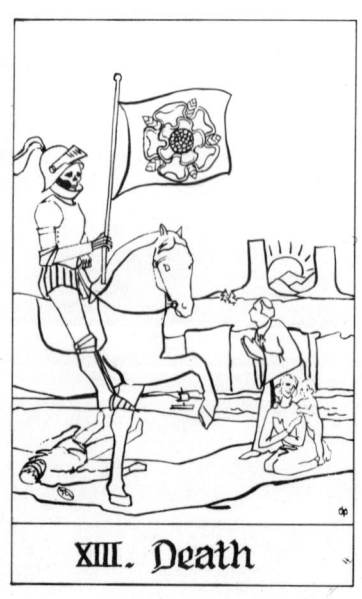

XIII. Death

XIV. Temperance

XV. The Devil

XVI. The Tower

XVII. The Star

XVIII. The Moon

XIX. The Sun

XX. Judgement

XXI. The Fool

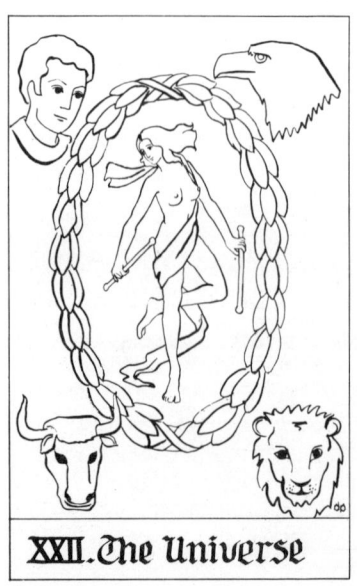

XXII. The Universe

The Major Arcana

ARCANUM I
THE MAGICIAN

A young man wearing a robe stands behind a table in a flower garden. His black hair is bound with a white band, symbolic of limited knowledge. Above his head is the symbol of infinity, the cosmic lemniscate shaped somewhat like the number 8 in a horizontal position, symbolizing eternal life. His belt is a serpent devouring its own tail, which signifies eternity. The Magician holds a scepter aloft in his right hand, while his left forefinger points to the earth. Thus he forms a channel, drawing power from above and directing it into manifestation on earth.

On the table before him are a cup, wand, sword, and pentacle, symbols of the Minor Arcana. These four articles represent the four natural elements of life: air, fire, water, and earth. All possibilities are there for his use as he progresses through the initiation of the Major Arcana.

The garden of roses and lilies signifies the cultivation of desires. The young man represents the personal will in union with the divine. He also represents self-consciousness (the self-conscious mind or the intellectual mind), the personality. As the Magician, he is not yet wed to the High Priestess or to the subconscious mind. He foreshadows submission of personal consciousness to the direction of the universal mind. He is in a state of self-surrender and derives all power from above.

The Hebrew letter for Arcanum I is aleph, which means "man." The equivalent English letter for aleph is *A*. The numerical value for this card is 1.

THE MEANING OF TAROT

DIVINATORY MEANING, UPRIGHT: This is the card of Will. It represents the creation of new things, the beginning of new projects, positive action, accepting changes in life that lead to success. It also signifies mastery, self-confidence, strong will power, skill, diplomacy, and initiative.

REVERSED: The use of power for destructive ends, a weak nature, indecision, failure of projects, bad luck in general. Also, putting success above warmth and love, which leads to unhappiness; self-centeredness, which blinds the individual to seeing anyone else clearly; trickery.

The Major Arcana

ARCANUM II
THE HIGH PRIESTESS

The High Priestess is seated on a cubic throne between two pillars with cube bases and lilybud tops (sometimes shown in its Eastern form of a lotus). The flower work at the top is the symbol of virginity and undeveloped power, showing that the full force of subconsciousness has not yet been reached in this card. There are the pillars of the Temple of Wisdom, which is the Temple of Solomon or Hermes. The High Priestess guards the entrance of the mysteries of all that is outside consciousness.

Tradition holds that the Temple of Solomon is the kingdom of heaven. The mystic sets out to rebuild the Temple or City of the Soul and to transform the dark chamber of his individual mind into a miniature Temple of the Holy Spirit (I. Cor. 3:16) and thus to become a nail, stone, or pillar in the greater cosmic Temple of King Solomon (Rev. 3:12). The Book of Kings describes the Temple building and states that Solomon set up two pillars on the porch and named the one on the right Jachin and that on the left Boaz. Upon the top of the pillars was lily work.

The black pillar to the right of the High Priestess has a white letter B (for Boaz) on it and represents the moon, the obvious, the negative force, the negative life principle, negation ("No", denial, refusal), resistance, and evil. The white pillar to her left has a black letter J (for Jachin) on it and represents the sun, the secret, the positive force, the positive life principle, affirmation ("Yes," confirmation), initiative, and good.

The veil or curtain between the pillars, forming a back-

THE MEANING OF TAROT

drop behind the High Priestess, conceals from view all that is outside consciousness, transcending the material universe. This means, then, that the veil opens into the realm of the subconscious. This veil may be the veil before the holy of holies, known as the *Paroketh*, which by wisdom "is rent from the top to the bottom."

The veil is decorated with palm and pomegranate symbols, suggesting the union of positive and negative forces and also indicating that the subconscious self or level can be released and used for creative activities and reproductive purposes only when focused impulses or mental drives originating at the self-conscious level pass through the veil or barrier to the subconscious level. In many of the languages of the world, the word *palm* is somehow connected with the sun, which is the male or positive force. On the other hand, the Song of Solomon (4:13) describes the garden of King Solomon's bride as "an orchard of pomegranates, with pleasant fruits." The pomegranate is a symbol of fertility and the female or negative force.

The High Priestess is wearing a flowing gown and robe of radiant light, for she is clothed with the sun. The bottom of her blue robe has the appearance of water from which flows the water of the spirit, wisdom, and consciousness. This stream of consciousness flows over into some of the other cards. She wears a horned-moon headdress consisting of a full moon set between the horns of Isis, which also looks like two crescent moons. This is the headdress worn by Isis when she received Osiris. It is the symbol of the generative power in nature, the regeneration of plants, and spring.

On her lap, the High Priestess holds a scroll inscribed with the word *Tora*, which is the divine law, the Tetra-

The Major Arcana

grammation, the universal principle that manifests itself in every sphere of life. The word *Tora* is also related to the word *Tarot* or the Book of *Thoth*. The scroll is also partly hidden beneath her robe, for only part of the mystery of the levels of existence can be comprehended at the beginning of the Tarot paths. This scroll is also the imperishable book of memory in which all thoughts and actions from the beginning of time are recorded. The subconscious reflects upon the memories stored in our inner selves, which have a profound effect upon our lives. A person should care about what he thinks and does, for even a careless thought can have a later effect or reaction in his life. The record of memory is also a storehouse for knowledge gained in meditation. This knowledge is gleaned from the memory whenever it is needed.

On the breast of the High Priestess is the square solar cross, the sign of the moon, showing union of the positive (male, upright portion) and negative (female, horizontal portion) life elements, and indicates her balancing function. This union is typified again in that the sign of the moon on her breast is in close harmony with her clothes of the sun. At her feet is a yellow crescent moon, indicating the subconscious activities of the mind.

The scene illustrated in Arcanum II is out-of-doors, for behind the High Priestess can be seen a large body of water and a distant shore.

The card is said to represent one or more of the following: Artemis or Isis, the ancient Egyptian mother and fertility goddess; the priestess of the Silver Star; the guardian of the door of the sanctuary; the priestess of the Temple of Thoth; the balancing force; the eternal She; the spirit of the mysteries; a direct link between the Above

THE MEANING OF TAROT

and the Below, between heaven and earth. Other Tarot scholars are of the opinion that the High Priestess is Tashitum, Nebo's wife, called "the Interceder." Still others think that the High Priestess represents Juno, the goddess of Roman mythology who was the protector of women and presided over maternity.

The High Priestess has also been identified with the goddess Hathor, who is sometimes regarded as identical with Isis and at other times as the mother of Isis. Like the High Priestess, Hathor is depicted with cow's horns. Other goddesses whose identity has been linked to the High Priestess are Luna, Sol's wife, who was said to have all secret powers at her command; Diana, the celibate huntress and goddess of the crescent moon; and the great Hecate of the Greek occult philosophy, patroness of all crossroads, who was the mistress of evil enchantments, dark power of the moon. She definitely is *not*, as some suppose, the mythical Pope Joan of the Roman Church.

The High Priestess and the Empress of Arcanum III are the same person in a different capacity, each symbolizing different things concerning the subconscious. The High Priestess symbolizes the virgin state of subconsciousness, which lacks stimulus to put it to use. The Empress symbolizes the impregnated state of subconsciousness, which has received stimulus originating from the Magician and introduced by the Emperor. The High Priestess has not yet united with the Emperor and is only potentially a mother of children or mental images. She is a symbol of the root substance that is the basis of all subconscious activity. She is High Priestess over the beginning of all subconscious activity.

In another respect the High Priestess is the highest feminine elder, the main receptive aspect of the "life-power." She is Prakriti of Hindu philosophy, the First Mother or First Matter, the primary root substance, the cosmic mind-stuff. She is also the Spiritual Bride and Mother, before her union with Adam. In connection with her function as Spiritual Bride, the High Priestess is the secret church.

The Hebrew letter for the second Arcanum is beth, which hieroglyphically expresses mouth or tongue, and has the numerical value of 2.

DIVINATORY MEANING, UPRIGHT: If the inquirer is a female, this card represents her in the Tarot fortune spread. If the inquirer is a male, this card represents a female presently in his life or who will be in his life at a later date. This card stands for mystery, secrets, the unrevealed future, tenacity, wisdom, science, hidden influences at work, fluctuation, and reaction.

REVERSED: The cards immediately surrounding the High Priestess have a negative effect on it. In the reversed position this card stands for conceit, the accepting of knowledge seen only on the surface, sensual enjoyment, selfishness, and ruthlessness.

THE MEANING OF TAROT
ARCANUM III
THE EMPRESS

A pregnant matronly woman is seated upon a cushioned throne. She is wearing a flowered gown, and her yellow hair is bound with a wreath of myrtle, a plant sacred to Venus. Her hair is loose about her shoulders, and she is crowned with twelve stars. Around her neck she wears a necklace of seven pearls, which are of Venus. She holds a scepter in her right hand. At the upper end of the scepter is a globe of the world surmounted by a Cross of Manifestation. An inverted tav is shown within the circle of the globe. Under her left foot is a silver crescent moon. A heart-shaped shield, decorated with the emblem of an eagle, rests against the right side of her throne. The eagle is the symbol of both the soul and life.

In the foreground is a cornfield while in back of the Empress, trees grow in a field of flowers. The river and waterfall in the midst of the flower garden symbolize the principle of generation. This river that waters the Empress's garden is the same stream of consciousness that begins in the robe of the High Priestess.

The Empress' attributions closely resemble the woman described in the Apocalypse of St. John (Rev. 12:1-2): "A seated woman clothed with the sun, and the moon under her feet, and upon her head a crown of twelve stars; and she being with child . . ."

The Empress has also been linked to the Egyptian goddess Isis, who was called Queen of Heaven in addition to Our Lady and Mother of God. She too was represented standing on the crescent moon and surrounded by twelve

The Major Arcana

stars. Isis was worshiped under different names in different provinces. At Thebes she was called Mut. In Bubastes she was known as Sekhet, and at Dendera she was Hathor. An old Latin spelling of the name is Ator.

The Empress is also said to represent Venus Urania of Roman mythology, or the Egyptian goddess Maat, the goddess of truth who is called Lady of Heaven and Giver of Life. Maat was the personification of original and celestial reason, and was regarded as the Great Mother. Her name was sometimes spelled Maut, Maht, and Mut. The Empress also may be identified with Ishtor of the Babylonians and Assyrians.

The Magician of Arcanum I, and the High Priestess of Arcanum II are united so that the Magician becomes the Emperor and the High Priestess becomes the Empress.

The Empress is the creative imagination, the creator of mental imagery. Since imagination originates in the subconscious, she represents the subconscious as the element generating mental images. As the Empress has control over her subjects, subconsciousness (the Empress) has control over the development of mental imagery in the material world. Thus, in a sense, the Empress symbolizes generation and productive forces. Whereas the High Priestess symbolizes the virgin state of the primary powers of subconsciousness, with a lack of stimulus to put these powers to use, the Empress symbolizes the impregnated state of the productive and generating activities of the Magician. The Empress has received stimulus from ideas originating at the subconscious level represented in Arcanum I. Now as the Emperor, he is the father of her children, mental images.

This concept is carried through in the Hebrew letter

THE MEANING OF TAROT

for this Arcanum, gimel, which means "the taking hand." The hieroglyph represents a hand making a loose fist so that it forms a narrow tunnel, which can take or receive something. Keeping in mind the impregnating function of the Empress' consort, this tunnel appears to represent the womb, which is the last station of the idea before birth as mental imagery.

Gimel is the equivalent of the English letter hard G and has the numerical value of 3. In the Zodiac, gimel corresponds to the Earth and symbolizes action.

DIVINATORY MEANING, UPRIGHT: This is a card of action. It predicts fruitfulness, beauty, luxury, pleasure, success, material wealth, contentment, marriage, fertility, fruitful projects, sound understanding of people and their problems, action and circulation, creation, spiritual insight, feminine sympathy, partnership, and night. If this card is badly placed in a spread, it means sensuality, dissipation, luxuriousness.

REVERSED: Inaction; using resources unwisely; possibility of broken home, due to poverty and famine; possible indication of war, destruction, or plague; fear; anxiety.

The Major Arcana
ARCANUM IV
THE EMPEROR

A regal, bearded man is seated upon a throne with his legs crossed which resembles the number 4 to form the hieroglyph of Jupiter, the star of this card. The number 4 represents the four elements—earth, air, fire, water—emblematic of all physical matter.

The Emperor's posture also indicates a triangle over a cross, which is the sign of alchemical Sulphur, and suggests the Athanor of the alchemists. Looking straight out of the picture, the Emperor wears a six-pointed crown with an Aries sign on top. In his right hand he holds a T-shaped scepter surmounted with a circle. This is the symbol of the lingam and the Egyptian ankh. The lingam (or lingan) in Hindu mythology is a phallus, symbol of Siva, a member of the Hindu trinity. The ankh is a symbol of enduring life or generation and combines the masculine and feminine elements. The scepter also represents the Cross of Life, the sight of which causes the powers of darkness to retreat. It draws truth and inspiration from above which breaks down structures of ignorance and false reasoning.

In his left hand, the Emperor holds a globe, which is the symbol of dominion. The arms and top corners of the throne are each decorated with a ram's head, the emblem of Mars. The Emperor's left shoulder-piece also has a ram's head.

The scene is out-of-doors, for in the background can be seen a river and barren mountains. The river is the same stream of consciousness that begins in the robes of the

THE MEANING OF TAROT

High Priestess. The mountains represent somber regulation and unyielding power. They are also symbols of the Great Work. The adept's aspiration will help him to reach their tops.

The Emperor is said to represent Jupiter or Amum, the Egyptian Amon, the Babylonian Marduk, and Merodach of the Bible. He is also called the Father. The great Temple of Amon was located in the southern Egyptian capital of Thebes. The meaning of the name Amon is to veil, to hide, concealment. One of the invocations to Amon begins "Hail to thee, Lord of Truth, whose shrine is hidden." In ancient Egypt Amon's most common title was Suten-Netern, king of the gods. He was also called Hek or Hyk, the Emperor, the Ruler, Lord of Heaven, Lord of Truth, Strong Bull. Amon's image, like that of this card, is represented as seated on a throne. He holds a scepter, symbolizing power and plenty.

The Emperor was the Magician of Arcanum I. He is now the Grand Architect of the Universe and the Ancient of Days and is the father of the Empress' children. He now has parental authority and hence, represents the paternal power. His throne signifies subconsciousness, which is the root substance that takes form as mental images. But the Emperor himself represents the intellect or self-consciousness of man. He is lord of thought and reason rather than of the emotions or the subconscious mind. Reason is the mental tool man uses to prepare for right action; reason stimulates the subconscious to produce mental images of a higher type. The Emperor sets the pattern in order. In this function he implies both authority and paternity.

Arcanum IV is represented by the Hebrew letter daleth

The Major Arcana

which connotes "thorax" or "nourishing breast." The general meaning is "fulfillment." The number is 4.

DIVINATORY MEANING, UPRIGHT: This is the card of realization. It signifies the use of good reason, a superior with a reasonable attitude, will power, the higher-intellect, stability, temporal power, a great person, aid, conviction, authority, leadership, mental activity, ambition, oversight, good control over passions, protection, support, realization of great plans, loyalty, competition, marriage, obstinacy.

REVERSED: Weak character, emotional immaturity, fear of authority, loss or lack of self-control, death in conflict or war, critical bodily injury, still under the authority of parents, possibility of losing inheritance due to defraud or thievery, possibility of household injury, possibility of injury due to misrepresented facts.

THE MEANING OF TAROT
ARCANUM V
THE HIEROPHANT

An interpreter of sacred mysteries and esoteric principles wearing the ecclesiastical attire of superior office is seated on a throne between two pillars which have fluted tops and phallic symbols of union. These pillars repeat the theme of the High Priestess in Arcanum II and represent the duality of law and liberty, united with the freedom of free will of man to seek the path of his own choosing. The pillars stand on either side of the path to spiritual attainment and esoteric knowledge. The back of the throne is decorated with the letter P surmounted with a trefoil (three-leaved ornament). The letter P signifies the All-Parent and in its form is related to the shepherd's crook. It also represents the crosier or pastoral staff which was used by the Druids and is still the symbol of a bishop or supreme ecclesiastical authority. It is the pastoral crook of the Good Shepherd of All Souls. The trefoil with its three golden spheres signifies the triple perfection: Gold is the perfect metal, the sphere or circle is the perfect form, and three is considered the perfect number.

The Hierophant is wearing a miter resembling the official headdress of the ancient Jewish high priest. The sides of the miter flare out slightly at the sides suggesting wings or horns. The top of the miter has a cross supporting three small spheres. The intimated wings or horns on either side of the small Circles of Perfection or Pearls of Price are symbolically guarding Good Thought, Good Deed, and Good Word. It is also the Crown of Life, the aspiration of man.

The Major Arcana

The right hand of the Hierophant is uplifted with two fingers raised making the sign of esotericism, which suggests that more exists than just what man can see with his eyes; some knowledge is hidden from the view of the masses.

In his left hand, the Hierophant holds a scepter with three crossbars, which is symbolic of his mastery in the three worlds of the physical, astral, and mental. Just below the Hierophant's throat at the top of his garment is a moon-shaped clasp. At his feet are crossed keys, one gold and one silver, representing the keys of the hidden doctrine.

Like the Israelite high priest, the Hierophant's robe is blue with a decorative hem of blue, purple and red pomegranates, interspersed with knots of golden cord. This description is similar to that given in Exodus (28:33-34).

A carpet covers the floor beneath the Hierophant's feet. The edge of the carpet is checkered with black and white, representing the manifestation of the life-power alternately as light and then darkness.

Two attendant priests dressed in robes are kneeling before the Hierophant. The robe of the priest to the left of the Hierophant is decorated with lilies. The other priest's robe is plain.

The illustration of Arcanum V includes a total of five crosses, including the cross atop the miter, the crossed keys, and the crosses of the triple-barred scepter. The number 5 is the pentagram of the Cabala and the flaming star of the gnostics.

Some scholars think there is a connection between the Hierophant and the Egyptian god Ptah, who was greatly revered and feared. Many temples were dedicated to the

THE MEANING OF TAROT

worship of this Egyptian god. The triple-barred scepter is a peculiar emblem associated with Ptah, who was called the Revealer, for he made hidden duties manifest.

There is also a connection with the ancient Hebrews, for the Hierophant blesses the two kneeling attendants with the uplifted palm in the manner sacred to Hebrew religious ceremonies. This gesture apparently was inherited from the "hand of the Cohen" of the Jews. Only the descendants of Aaron (Cohen) could bestow benediction in this manner.

The Hierophant is not the overseer or highest authority of the traditional religion of the masses or any other esoteric external doctrine. As the chief expounder of the esoteric doctrine, he is concerned only with the initiated, for whom he offers a passageway between the external experience and inner illumination. He represents intuition. When the subconscious responds to reason, the result is intuition. He speaks to those who have "ears" to hear the "inner voice" and reveals to them sacred concepts, and the significance of the appearance all around them. Intuition may come in the form of inspiration or direct revelation.

The accompanying Hebrew letter for Arcanum V is heh, which means "aspiration" or "breath." The English letter for heh is *H* as in hour, or *E*. The numerical value is 5.

DIVINATORY MEANING, UPRIGHT: This is the card of mercy. If the inquirer is a male this card represents him in the Tarot fortune spread (layout). If the inquirer is a female this card represents a male in her life. Preference for ritual, creed, the outer forms of religion; bondage to social conventions, need to conform, to be approved by

The Major Arcana

society; intuition; teaching; inspiration; possibility of a marriage or alliance; occult force, voluntarily called upon; mercy and goodness; service to mankind; captivity; the wise man you turn to for advice in solving a problem; self-mastery; reunion.

REVERSED: Unconventionality, unorthodoxy, openness to new ideas, gullibility, superstitious fears, doubt, renunciation of religion, divorce, kindness, and weakness.

ARCANUM VI
THE LOVERS

A naked man is standing under a tree, which is bearing twelve fiery fruits in the shape of triple flames. He looks toward a nude woman who is standing beneath a tree, which is bearing five circular fruits. A serpent is entwined in the tree.

The woman stands looking at an angel who appears in the huge sunburst dominating the top half of the card. His arms are outstretched as if in a blessing.

A conical hill or mountain is in the center background. It represents the peak to which man aspires and prepares to reach in the future.

The man represents Adam and is also linked with the Magician of Arcanum I, for he is the self-conscious intellect. The woman represents Eve and is also linked with the High Priestess of Arcanum II and the Empress of Arcanum III, for she is the subconscious. The angel represents the archangel Raphael, angel of air, and the archangel of the eastern quarter of heaven. He signifies superconsciousness. The female (the inner interpreting subconscious) receives the stimulus of the male (the outer observing self-conscious). This union of the self-conscious with the subconscious is mystical love and is the way to obtain the blessing of Raphael, superconsciousness. Another way of stating this principle is that the self-conscious intellect must oblige the subconscious if it is to establish direct contract with superconsciousness. While this is taking place, the angel pours down his blessing or influence of creative power on the Lovers below.

The Major Arcana

The yellow or golden sun offers potential consciousness as it provides energy and life. The tree bearing the twelve triple fruits or flames is the Tree of Life, which is really the tree of human life. The twelve fruits stand for the twelve signs of the Zodiac, and the twelve main types of human personality which is actually the self-conscious intellect. The triple flames stand for the subdivision of the Zodiac into three decanates, and the thirty-six subtypes of self-conscious intellect or personality.

The tree bearing five circular fruits is the Tree of the Knowledge of Good and Evil. The five fruits represent the five senses. The serpent is the subconscious memory of sensation, who climbs the tree bringing temptation.

Arcanum VI appears to have no connection with any of the occult gods of either Egypt or Babylonia. However, the story of Adam and Eve as pictured in this card was known in Babylonia long before it was revealed to the writer of Genesis.

The Hebrew letter for Arcanum VI is vav, which is the hieroglyphic sign for eyes, light, or brilliancy. The English letters for vav are *V, U,* and *V.* The corresponding number is 6.

DIVINATORY MEANING, UPRIGHT: This card represents predicaments and predicts fulfillment of the inquirer's dreams and desires if it is placed in the divinatory spread near a success card. This is the card of harmony. Choice between rival interests causing predicament; struggle between loyalty to one's mate and a desire for others. Attraction, beauty, love, harmony of inner and outer life. The power of choice means responsibility, desire for pleasure of the spirit, love and passion, attraction, beauty of

THE MEANING OF TAROT

body and soul, trials overcome, artist wedded to his art, discrimination, choice, affection, and indecisions.

REVERSED: Parental interference in marriage, danger of infidelity, divorce and lawsuits, loss of love, possibility of wrong choice; feeling of inadequacy in fulfilling everyday responsibilities, failure, foolish desires, frustrations in marriage, creative dry spells.

The Major Arcana

ARCANUM VII
THE CHARIOT

A fair-haired king is standing under a canopy in a cubical Chariot drawn by two horses, symbols of the sun. The canopy is supported by four posts and is decorated with stars, symbols of the celestial forces. The king's crown is a triple-pentagram surmounted with an eight-pointed gold star. The scepter in his right hand is topped with a globe, a square, and a triangle. The defensive covering over his chest is decorated with three approximately right-angled bands. His shoulder-pieces are in visaged moon form, representing Urim and Thummin. The face of the one on his right shoulder is frowning, while that on his left is smiling. The king's skirt divides into eight segments covered with geometric symbols, typifying dominion over terrestrial forces. His belt, also containing mystic symbols, is slanting downward over his left hip. This slanting position symbolizes the slanting circle of the ecliptic. On the front of the Chariot appears the Hindu lingam surmounted by the flying globe of the Egyptians.

The charioteer is the man pictured in Arcanum VI, who is now progressing in triumph on the road to adeptship. He has successfully harnessed his divine and human natures. However, he still must control his worldly and spiritual urges if he is successfully to handle the responsibilities and trials that lie ahead. He holds the horses by the reins of his will.

The canopy represents the celestial forces. The four columns supporting the canopy signify the fourfold hermetic maxim: "To Dare, to be Silent, to Know, and to

THE MEANING OF TAROT

Try." The Chariot is the Chariot of the Sun and is identical to the Chariot of Fire mentioned in the Second Book of Kings. It represents the human personality, and is the vehicle of cosmic forces or universal will. When the human will is receptive to the universal will, the cosmic influences are manifested in thought and word.

The Hebrew letter for this card is sayir, which means "arrow," "sword," or "weapon." The English equivalent is Z. The numerical value is 7.

DIVINATORY MEANING, UPRIGHT: This is the card of Triumph and Victories (conquests) at all levels—in the mind and spirit, in science and art, in progress, in the battles of life; conquest; success for those engaged in artistic pursuits; triumph over money difficulties, ill health, and foes; promise of material success; possible reconciliation of separated or divorced inquirer; mastery of yourself, big achievement(s); ambitious greed. If the inquirer resists motives and subdues his animal passions, he will find advantage in his life and work; travel in safety (and comfort); recovery from any grave illness.

REVERSED: Sudden collapse of a project on the brink of success, decadent desires, perhaps an unethical victory, vengeance; riot, dispute, lawsuit, defeat; illness, general misfortune; restlessness, shrinking responsibilities, and reality.

The Major Arcana

ARCANUM VIII
JUSTICE

A yellow-haired woman is seated on a throne between two pillars. She holds aloft a double-edged sword in her right hand and suspends her balanced scales of judgment in her left hand. She wears no blindfold, for she is the personification of Spiritual Justice. Her crown has three turrets on top and is ornamented with a square jewel in the front. A veil behind the woman is stretched between the two pillars, which open into the realm of the superconscious. All knowledge is in the superconscious behind the veil. This figure of Justice has been compared to the Greek goddess Themis, who also was represented as holding a pair of scales in which she weighed the claims of mortals.

The figure of Justice represents one aspect of the productive powers of the creative imagination at work. The seated woman on this card symbolizes Justice and Mercy; Arcanum XI (Strength) represents another aspect of this operation. The double-edged sword tells us that action is required to penetrate the veil hiding All Knowledge. The scales signifies harmony, equilibrium, and a balanced personality, which is the result of right reason.

The Hebrew letter for this card is kheth, which means "a field." The English equivalent is *ch*. The numerical value is 8.

DIVINATORY MEANING, UPRIGHT: This is the card of Justice. A balanced personality; legal aspects of money matters with good outcome; the elimination of useless,

THE MEANING OF TAROT

outworn forms of education; a mixture of the right ingredients, as in science, chemistry, or cooking. It may mean education, with a well-balanced mind as its aim; justice and equity, harmony, law; strength and force, but arrested as in the act of judgment; legal affairs, lawsuits, when the question relates to material affairs; balance; peace.

REVERSED: Predicts all the bad aspects of law and legal complications; severity in judgment; injustice, inequality, legal complications, bias, excessive severity; false accusations, lawlessness, rioting, violence; bigotry. When this card is reversed and near Arcanum XII, The Hanged Man, it means mercy and forgiveness rather than severity.

The Major Arcana

ARCANUM IX
THE HERMIT

A bearded old man stands on a snowy mountain peak holding up a lantern in his right hand, thereby lighting the way for unseen climbers below. The light in his lantern is a six-pointed star. This light is spiritual truth and inspiration which crumbles the framework of ignorance and false reasoning. The Hermit's left hand rests on his staff, his will power.

He stands at the pentacle, above all things, which is the goal of existence. He is the foundation of all manifestation, the Absolute Wisdom, the Great Unknown, the Ancient of Days, the Supreme Will.

This state of being is the highest result of subconscious response to the initiative and the suggestions of self-consciousness or intellectual mind. Self-training and careful control of subconsciousness ultimately result in union with the Supreme Will. When this happens, all sense of self is lost, and aloneness with JHVH, Ain-Soph, the Absolute prevails.

The Hebrew letter for this card is teth, which means "a snake" (wisdom) or "protection given by wisdom and forethought." The English equivalent is *th* or *T*. The numerical value is 9.

DIVINATORY MEANING, UPRIGHT: This is the card of Prudence. This card predicts a meeting with one who will guide the inquirer on the path to material or spiritual goals, attainment, possible journey, caution, care, obstacles, intelligence.

THE MEANING OF TAROT

REVERSED: Immaturity, childishness, refusal to accept advancement in position or age and the accompanying responsibilities; foolish acts, ignorance; evasion of responsibilities; disguise, fear, unreasonable caution.

The Major Arcana

ARCANUM X
THE WHEEL OF FORTUNE

In the center of the card is a large circle enclosing another circle with a much smaller circle or hub inside that. Eight spokes radiate from the center of the hub to the middle circle. Four of these spokes are decorated with symbols at the outer tips. The one pointing to the Sphinx sitting on top of the wheel is the alchemical sign of mercury. The Sphinx is wearing a kingly headdress and holds a double-edged sword over his left shoulder.

The symbol on the spoke pointing to the Egyptian god Hermes-Anubis, who is ascending the right side of the wheel, is the sign of sulphur. The symbol on the spoke pointing to Typhon, who is descending the left side of the wheel, is the sign for salt. Typhon or Set is the evil genius of Egyptian mythology. Straight downward at the feet of Hermes-Anubis is the alchemical sign of Aquarius, symbol of water (dissolution).

The word *TARO* is interspersed around the wheel between the figures on the outer circle and the alchemical signs just inside the middle circle. The *T* is above the sign of mercury; the *A* is outside the sign of sulphur; the *R* is on the outside of the water sign; and the *O* is outside the sign of salt.

At the corners of the card are the heads of the mystic animals mentioned in Ezekiel (1:10) and Revelation (4:7). The eagle in the upper right corner corresponds to the fixed sign of the Zodiac called Scorpio. The lion in the lower right corner corresponds to the Leo sign. The bull in the lower left corner corresponds to Taurus. And

THE MEANING OF TAROT

the man or angel in the upper left corner corresponds to Aquarius.

This card stresses the active participation of man the microcosm in his destiny. He must look within himself and use his psychic forces to control his life and destiny, rather than allowing himself to be controlled by it. The king of Arcanum VI now enjoys a spiritual triumph. He realizes that the alternating phases in the course of fate are not as capricious as they seem. He also knows that the Wheel of Fate or Fortune is only one of the many instruments of destiny; it is not destiny itself. Hence, all influences and their processes are reciprocal.

The Hebrew letter for Arcanum X is yod (jod), which means "the open hand," indicating power, or "the forefinger extended as a sign of command." The English equivalent is Y. The numerical value is 10.

DIVINATORY MEANING, UPRIGHT: This is the card of Fortune. Fate and the more fortunate spins of the wheel, success in your chosen career, luck, happiness in the work you do everyday. This card predicts growth, predicts prosperity after famine and success after failure. Good fortune, success, increase; unexpected turn of luck.

REVERSED: Fortune will have its ups and downs; there may be a turn for the worse; hard luck at every turn; you will reap as you have sown; easy success and plenty followed by a fall.

ARCANUM XI
STRENGTH

A woman is confidently closing the mouth of a lion. Resembling a horizontal 8, the infinity sign, the cosmic lemniscate, symbol of eternal life, is seen over the woman's head. Her hair is bound with a floral wreath. Her dress is decorated with trifoliate crosses.

The terrain is rough, and trees and mountains can be seen in the distance. The sky is clear.

This card represents one phase of the productive powers of the creative imagination at work. Arcanum VIII represents another phase. The first enlightenment of the Magician of Arcanum I is manifest in this card as the divine will in operation, demonstrating the domination of spiritual over physical power. Thus the woman, sometimes called the Enchantress, conquers the gnostic Lion-Serpent, Nahash, the Guardian of the Threshold. The operative will power of the initiate is now under the control of his spiritual intelligence.

Whereas the growth processes of involution began with Arcanum I, the process of evolution begins with Arcanum XI. Therefore, this card marks the halfway ascent of the initiate in the Major Arcana.

The Enchantress has been linked with Una; Virgo the Mother; the eternal She; and often considered to be a female equivalent of St. George and the Dragon.

The Hebrew letter for Arcanum XI is kaph, which typifies "a grasping hand" or "a curve." The English equivalent is *K*. The numerical value is 20, but as a final letter, 500.

THE MEANING OF TAROT

DIVINATORY MEANING, UPRIGHT: This is the card of Spiritual Strength. A male having this card in his spread will have a female in his life with the qualities of the woman pictured on this card. A female having this card in her spread has a strength and ability to overcome suffering through patience and the application of her femininity to everyday problems. Spiritual power will overcome material power; love will triumph over hate, the higher nature over carnal desires; power and action in life, courage and magnanimity, power, control of the life-force; inner strength, energy; victory over evil; struggle for supremacy; success and honors.

REVERSED: The abuse of power, the domination of the material, discord; emotional instability, possible financial destruction; weakness of character, physical illness, impotence, bad temper that will cause others grief, typranny, disgrace.

The Major Arcana

ARCANUM XII
THE HANGED MAN

A white-haired man is suspended by one foot from a beam supported by two lopped tree trunks, each with six lopped branches. His head hangs over a pit, and his left leg is crossed behind the right one. His hands are behind the upper part of his back so that the arms form a triangle. His left ankle is bound to the tau cross with what appears to be a supple branch of the crosspiece. The appearance of the cross above the peculiar posture of the man suggests a cross on top of a water triangle.

In this position, the man represents the Ancient of Days reflected in the personality. He is suspended and dependent upon the All. The upside-down position represents a reversal of the mind from the things in this world. He has disciplined himself and completely surrendered the personal life, the personal consciousness, to the superior will of life itself, the universal mind. He is now aware that his personality is the channel through which the forces of the universe carry on the Great Work.

The Hebrew letter for Arcanum XII is lamed, which means "to instruct." The English letter for lamed is *L*. The numerical value is 30.

DIVINATORY MEANING, UPRIGHT: This is the card of Sacrifice. In spiritual matters, wisdom that comes from trials and sacrifice, surrender to a higher being causes a reversal in one's way of life; intuition and the power of prophecy, prudence, self-sacrifice. It may also mean sus-

THE MEANING OF TAROT

pended decisions, a pause in one's life. In material affairs: losses, reverses, anxiety, victim of intrigues of others.

REVERSED: Absorption in physical matters; preoccupation with the ego; resistance to spiritual influences, arrogance, selfishness; false prophecy.

The Major Arcana

ARCANUM XIII
DEATH

A skeleton wearing defense body protection rides upon a white horse. The skeleton is holding a banner displaying the Mystic Rose. A king lies dead beneath the horse's hoofs. A woman and a child kneel helpless before the figure, while a strong man vainly stands in the rider's path. In the immediate background, a boat is floating on a river. This is symbolic of the River Styx and its ferry.

Behind the river, a steep precipice rises to a beautiful land, where two pillarlike towers frame the mountains and rising sun in the distance. This scene beyond the river represents the other side of death, which is birth. Death is birth to another kind of life. Therefore, the Divine Wisdom riding his white horse over the field of subconsciousness is the manifestation of Freedom.

But this card represents death of the old self, not physical death. In Arcanum XII, the initiate had passed through the fleshly desires and temptation of youth and reversed his mind, aspiring to an ethical future. In Arcanum XIII, the initiate experiences a transforming force or regeneration of the soul. He has now learned of the more serious affairs of life. The image of Death is the halfway position in the Major Arcana. This central position indicates the dividing period in a man's life.

The Hebrew letter for Arcanum XIII is mem, which means "fertility," "formation," or "seas." The English letter for mem is *M*. In occultism there is a similarity between the words *fertility* and *seas*. The numerical value is 40. When mem is a final letter, the value is 600.

THE MEANING OF TAROT

DIVINATORY MEANING, UPRIGHT: This is the card of Change. This is the card of failures, endings, possible death and destruction. It predicts a great sudden change in the inquirer's life. The cards surrounding this one in a spread will clarify the nature of the change. If it is next to a Court card representing someone other than the inquirer, he will be affected by a change as a result of his relationship with that other person. This card further predicts transformation, sometimes destruction followed or preceded by transformation; despair giving way to or preceded by hope and better things; a change or altercation, which may be in the form of consciousness; sometimes it may mean birth and renewal (rebirth), the conclusion of a part of the inquirer's life and the beginning of a new period of experiences; it may suggest the death of a person or it may indicate "dying" many times in life's experiences before real death occurs rather than finality; depression.

REVERSED: Possibility of unfortunate combinations; competing interests in business or personal affairs; lethargy, sleep; destroyed hope; or birth, broken home restored; order following chaos; the appearance of new enterprise in the near future.

ARCANUM XIV
TEMPERANCE

A yellow-haired angel is pouring liquid (the essences of life) from a golden chalice in his left hand to a silver one in his right hand. The solar disk on his brow illuminates his head. Over the breast of his gown, he wears a triangle in a square. The angel is standing with his left foot next to irises on dry land and his right foot in the pool of water in the foreground. A path from the pool leads across undulating country to a line of mountains. The sun just above the mountain peaks is shaped like a spectral crown. A rainbow is in the sky on the other side of the angel.

The angel has been identified with Iris, who was a privileged messenger of the gods, and with the archangel Michael. Diana, the huntress, has also been linked with the angel, because of the reference of the rainbow to Sagittarius and the Bow of Promise. And yet another goddess has been identified with the angel. The Egyptian goddess Nut or Hephthys was known as the Elder, the mother of the Gods, and the Nurse. She is usually represented as pouring a liquid from a vase. The angel is probably Raphael, however.

The word *temperance* in Arcanum XIV refers to tempering or bringing something to a proper state by blending, or a mixture. It also means the modification of the properties of something by adding another substance to it. The angel is pouring the spirit into matter, which modifies the matter. The pool is the reservoir of the substance of mind. Hence, the action of the angel also represents the pouring

THE MEANING OF TAROT

of the substance of mind (universal consciousness) from the past, through the present, into the future. Thus the Guardian Angel is there to assist the initiate along the path toward attainment. This card also signifies the union of the male and female principles.

The crown at the end of the path signifies the number 1, or mastery. The Hebrew letter for Arcanum XIV is nun, literally, "fish," which can also mean "fruit of any kind" or "all things produced." The English letter for nun is N. The numerical value is 50; as a final letter, 700.

DIVINATORY MEANING, UPRIGHT: This is the card of combination. Good management in business and personal life, self-control, discipline, economy, moderation, frugality, temperance, adaptation, coordination, modification; the use of successful combinations; the individualization of existence; diplomacy; delay; change, reconciliation, or remarriage; the minister who joins the male and female principles in the union of wedlock is Temperance personified; completion of all projects in time; all physical and mental pursuits will be fruitful and bring the inquirer a balanced life.

REVERSED: Possibility of unfortunate combinations; competing interests in business or personal affairs; low-grade desires and actions, hostility, fighting and separation, sterility, unfulfillment of all desires, fanaticism, unhappy union, competing interests.

The Major Arcana

ARCANUM XV
THE DEVIL

A goat-headed devil with batlike wings is sitting on an elevated half-cube, possibly in a quagmire. The half-cube symbolizes half-knowledge, that is, the half of knowledge that is "visible," the sensory side of existence. The pentagram between the Devil's horns signifies that he represents the reversal of man's rightful place in the universe. Thus, the Devil represents the opposite of the Angel in Arcanum VI. The legs of the Devil are hairy like those of an animal, and his feet are talons. Although his bare chest is male in character, the heavy hair on his lower extremities hides his female aspect. He lifts his right hand in a sign of duality, while he holds an inverted torch downward with his left hand. In this position, the torch is a sign of destruction. Two nude human figures wearing horned headdress are tied by their necks with loose-fitting chains to a ring bolt in the front of the Devil's pedestal. The figure with a flame-ended tail is a man and the one with a pomegranate-tipped tail is a woman. The remainder of the card is in total darkness.

The Devil is also known as the Black Magician and is the antithesis of the Magician of Arcanum I. The Devil should not be rigidly equated with Satan or the esoteric importance of this card would not be fully appreciated. The Devil is also the opposite of the Angel in Arcanum VI. The initiate was raised to angelic heights in Arcanum XIV and acquired control over the Astral Light. But the Devil, the polar opposite of everything in nature, opposes man's struggle for freedom. The initiate must take care

THE MEANING OF TAROT

not to let pride, conceit, and lust for domination cause him to put his magical powers to evil use.

This card also symbolizes opposition to man's struggle for freedom. Ignorance and limitation are the causes of bondage. In false knowledge, subconscious motives are permitted to dominate the personality.

The Hebrew letter for Arcanum XV is *samekh*, which means "prop." The English equivalent is the *S* sound. The numerical value is 60.

DIVINATORY MEANING, UPRIGHT: This is the card of Fate. Domination of matter over spirit; sensation divorced from understanding; illness, bondage to the material, disease, violence, rage, fury, brute force, revolution, necessity, extraordinary effort, fate, black magic; undercurrent, lack of principle, disregard for human dignity, relentless drive to achieve power and wealth by cruel means and dishonesty if necessary, but such gain will eventually be lost; perverse personality.

REVERSED: The beginning of spiritual understanding; a physical healing has started; tendency to ineffectuality, indecision; death by evil means, weakness, timidity, blindness; petty, spiteful, lazy, lack of drive and the will for personal success and improvement; not necessarily a bad person, but one who is useless to himself and society. Often holds sentimental attitude toward life.

The Major Arcana
ARCANUM XVI
THE TOWER

A tower on top of a high pinnacle is being struck by lightning, which separates the top of the Tower from the rest of the structure. This falling top is in the shape of a crown with four constellations. The sky is cloudy, but the lightning flash issues from the sun.

The Tower has twenty-two courses of masonry, emblematic of the twenty-two Hebrew letters or the twenty-two cards of the Major Arcana. Near the top of the structure there are three windows, one over two, with flames appearing out of them.

Two human figures surrounded by a total of twenty-two small flames or yods, are falling to the ground. The falling man on the left side of the picture is accompanied by twelve yods, and the falling woman is accompanied by ten yods. A yod, sometimes called "a drop of light," stands for power, skill, and dexterity. It also represents the descent of the life-force or Solar Spirit into matter or the conditions of material existence. It corresponds to the Zodiacal sign of the Virgin.

The lightning represents a quick, momentary look at spiritual truth. It is a flash of inspiration that crumbles the framework of ignorance and false reasoning, which bound the man and woman in Arcanum XV. This flash of right knowledge overcomes the combination of the emotions and subconscious motives over the personality.

The Hebrew letter for this card is ayin, which means "eye" or "foundation." The English equivalent is the letter O. The numerical value is 70.

THE MEANING OF TAROT

DIVINATORY MEANING, UPRIGHT: This is the card of Ruin. Overthrow of existing modes of life; conflict, unforeseen catastrophe; old nations upset; selfish ambition about to fall, bankruptcy; danger, poverty.

REVERSED: The same as above in a lesser degree. Oppression, imprisonment, tyranny, false accusations.

The Major Arcana

ARCANUM XVII
THE STAR

A young naked woman is kneeling with her left knee on the ground and her right foot upon a pool of water. She pours the Waters of Life impartially from two pitchers. The one in her left hand pours onto the earth, which represents matter. The one in her right hand pours into the pool, which represents universal consciousness.

The ibis sitting on the tree in the background represents the soul resting in the Tree of Life. A mountain can be seen in the distance. In the sky is a huge Star surrounded by seven smaller ones. All of the stars have eight points each.

The maiden represents Mother Nature and eternal youth and beauty. The card represents the Waters of Life flowing freely and perpetually renewing creation.

The Hebrew letter is peh, which means "the tongue" or "the mouth as an organ of speech." The corresponding English letter is P. The numerical value is 80, but as a final letter, 800.

DIVINATORY MEANING, UPRIGHT: This is the card of Hope. In a spread this card represents a person who will come into the inquirer's life and have a lifelong affect upon him. This is more pronounced if the inquirer is a woman, for this other person will become the most important person she has ever met. Hope, strength, insight, courage, a bright future, promising outlook, inspiration; no destruction is final; unselfish aid will be given; good health; spiritual love; influence over others; new mental

THE MEANING OF TAROT

and spiritual perception, heightened intuition, potency.

REVERSED: Storms will be weathered, peace gained at a cost; imagination will be harnessed by practical considerations; bad luck or disaster; despair, impotence, self-importance, arrogance, physical and mental illness.

The Major Arcana

ARCANUM XVIII
THE MOON

A dog and a wolf standing on either side of a path are barking at the waxing moon, which contains the profile of a human head. The Moon has thirty-two rays, sixteen long ones interspaced with sixteen shorter ones. Eighteen dewdrops, in the shape of yods, are falling from the Moon.

In the foreground, a crayfish is crawling from a pool of water onto a path that leads over a distant mountain peak. To travel the length of the path, the crayfish must first pass between the dog on the left and the wolf on the right, and between two towers in the background. At the water's edge, stones and plants are on either side of the crayfish.

The crayfish represents the early stages of conscious development, emerging from the pool of universal consciousness. The path ascending upward between the towers symbolizes the upward progress of man. It has been well worn by other travelers. The wolf signifies the untamed creatures of the animal kingdom, while the dog represents the tamed creatures. The stones and plants represent the mineral and the vegetable kingdoms.

The Moon symbolizes the reflected light of subconsciousness. The falling drops of dew represent the life-force descending into material existence.

This card represents the truth that even though the material human body cannot exercise the powers of an adept, it can be organized to become a vehicle for those powers.

The Hebrew letter for this card is tsadi, which means

THE MEANING OF TAROT

"an end" or "a fishhook." The English equivalent is *Ts*, *Tz*, or *Cz*. The numerical value is 90, but as a final letter, 900.

DIVINATORY MEANING, UPRIGHT: This is the card of Danger. If this card is placed in a bad position in the spread it predicts that a great mental instability will result in insanity. If the card is placed in a good position, it means peace, fruition of visions, calmness, victory over mental anguish, freedom from fear. Imagination, intuition, dreams; predicts unforeseen perils to those you love; unforeseen perils, deception, secret foes, disappointment, danger, occult forces, voluntary change.

REVERSED: Storms will be weathered, peace of mind gained at a cost; imagination will be harnessed by practical considerations; impermanence, inconstancy.

The Major Arcana

ARCANUM XIX
THE SUN

Two naked, fair-haired, preadolescent children are holding hands as they dance in a ring marked on the ground. Inside this ring is a smaller one, in which the boy's left foot is planted, and the girl's right. She is holding the boy's left hand with her right one. Their free hands are extended downward at arm's length, the arms form right angles to their bodies. The palm of the girl's left hand is turned palm downward. The boy's right hand is turned palm upward, as though he expects to receive something.

A huge Sun with a human face shines above the wall which is immediately behind the children. The Sun has eight pointed rays, eight secondary rays, and forty-eight tertiary rays. Six golden drops are falling on each side of the couple, and a seventh falls between them. The wall is composed of five courses of stone. Four sunflowers garland the wall, and another one in bud is turned toward the Sun.

The children represent perfect balance and control between consciousness (self-consciousness, the intellectual mind) and subconsciousness. Their clasped hands show that the activities of the two forms of human personality are in rhythmic harmony and perfect union here. Their nakedness illustrates their Eden-like innocence. They have not yet become fully polarized sexually. The wall encloses the Garden of Eden. The four sunflowers in full bloom correspond to the mineral, vegetable, animal, and human kingdoms, which are the four divisions of nature. They

THE MEANING OF TAROT

are turned toward the children, signifying that all creation turns to the human creature for its final development. The bud turned toward the Sun represents the small company of human beings in the Fifth Kingdom of the Spiritual Israel, who have given themselves over to complete dependence on the universal life-power.

The Sun signifies the conscious energy of the material forces of nature which are human in character and capabilities.

The Hebrew letter is koph, which means "a defensive weapon" or "back of the head." It corresponds to the English letter *K*. The numerical value is 100.

DIVINATORY MEANING, UPRIGHT: This is the card of Material Happiness. Happiness and material wealth, gain, riches; a good marriage and happy reunions; achievement in art, science and agriculture; studies completed, liberation; pleasure in the simple life, contentment, good health, good future.

REVERSED: The same as above in a lesser degree. Future plans clouded; possible broken engagement; loss of a valued object unless vigilance is exerted; voided contract; meet failure at every turn; a difficult childbirth.

ARCANUM XX
JUDGMENT

A winged angel emerges from a luminous cloud in the heavens and blows on a trumpet, which has an attached banner.

In the scene below, three naked human figures stand looking up at the angel from open coffins floating upon a body of rippling water. The woman in the coffin at the left is turned toward the man in the coffin at the right. The man is turned toward the woman. The child in the coffin between the man and the woman has his back to us. The woman's arms are extended in front of her. The child's arms are extended at 45-degree angles. The man has his arms crossed over his chest. Mountains line the distant shore.

The angel is Gabriel, the angel of the element water, and here represents the Divine Breath or cosmic fire. He blows on the trumpet and produces the creative Word which frees man from the limitations characteristic of his mundane world. The banner with the cross symbolizes that the correlation of the celestial with the terrestrial in the personal consciousness of the adept is now complete. This is a prelude to complete adeptship. The mountains represent the heights of abstract thought.

The Hebrew letter for this card is resh, which means "the head" or "the face." The English equivalent is R. The numerical value is 200.

DIVINATORY MEANING, UPRIGHT: This is the card of Result. Awakening, rebirth, change of position, renewal,

THE MEANING OF TAROT

regeneration of mind or body, new beginning; spiritual advancement or attainment; a change in personal consciousness which is now on the verge of blending with the universal; decision; a favorable legal judgment or, in some readings, a complete loss by lawsuit.

REVERSED: Failure to find happiness in old age; fear of death; divorce or separation, disillusionment, weakness, simplicity, deliberation, decision; physical health must be watched; possible loss of worldly goods; eye, ear, or heart disease.

ARCANUM XXI
THE FOOL

A young, innocent-looking youth is about to walk off a precipice into an abyss. He appears to be oblivious to his surroundings. He is on a mountain peak, judging from the other peaks in the background, which are either on a level with him or below him. A domesticated dog is bounding joyfully at the youth's feet. A serpent in the dust is crawling away in the opposite direction from the youth. The sky is free of clouds and the sun is shining behind the two strolling figures.

The youth's yellow hair is bound with a green wreath, which has a feather in it. He holds a silver rose in his left hand, and in his right hand he carries a staff, which is slung over his right shoulder. A wallet with a curious-looking eye painted on it is suspended from the upper end of the pole.

The youth's toga is decorated with a system of eight-spoked wheels with trefoils, a star, a crescent, a circle with a triple flame, a globe, and an unembellished circle. The toga is a brilliant white, reflecting the light of Universal Consciousness (God). At the level of consciousness (super-consciousness) the youth has now attained, the soul proceeds to direct vision of the Divine Light. The serpent belt around the youth's waist is the Serpent of Eternity.

The silver rose the youth carries is the symbol of love, the Heavenly Spirit, and the Ever-Existent Fires, and indicates self-conscious intellect. Prior to Christianity, the rose was identified with the Virgin Sophia. The staff represents the youth's will power. He does not have to lean on it for support or hold it cautiously as does the Hermit in Arcanum IX.

The wallet is the sum total of all the youth's experiences and subconscious memories; it is known as karma in Hindu philosophy. That is all he can take with him from this world. The symbol on his wallet represents the All-Seeing Eye familiar to Freemasonry, and the Eye of Horus in Egyptian occultism. Now that the superconscious is in control, the human vision is supplanted by inner vision. This inner awareness overreaches the bounds of human awareness, the material world. When the youth reaches the abyss he will have access to the treasure of experience stored in the universal memory. Both the staff and the wallet are attributes of the god Mercury.

The dog at the youth's heels represents the world, which could attack him. But the youth, who has mastered the world, pays no heed, for he knows that the world is really only looking for a master. As the opposite of worldly ways are the ways of God; dog spelled backward is God.

The serpent crawling away in the dust behind the youth signifies the earth's creeping attitude of materialism, from which the youth is walking away and leaving behind.

The circular sun over the youth's shoulder is the symbol of the Ever-Existent Great O, the Great Light of the Orb of God.

The youth is androgynous: both male and female. He represents superconsciousness, who has ascended the mountains which were pictured in the other cards and were the goal of his human vision. Now he is stepping out into the abyss of immeasurable space and eternity, the state of universal consciousness of the Ever-Existent Father, the great I Am, the combined past, present, and

The Major Arcana

future form of the verb "to be." In the abyss, the youth will become one with the Ever-Existent.

The word *abyss* is frequently applied to God and is fundamentally made up of *Ab is*, which means "God is" and is the same as "I Am," the Hebrew tetragrammation. So, the abyss is Universal Consciousness or God. When the youth (superconsciousness) reaches the abyss, he joins with Universal Consciousness. The symbolism of the youth's toga signifies this union that is soon to take place.

The number of the youth is 0, which is the same figure used in occultism for God, the Ever-Existent Great O, the Great *Sun*, or the Great One. Both the zero and the letter *o* are circles, one of the symbols on the youth's toga. Another symbol on his toga is a globe, which represents the Great Orb of God, or the Great Light of the Orb of God. The syllable *ob*, meaning "a ball," used to be synonymous with *orb*, the symbol of the youth. *Ab*, the Hebrew term for Father (God) is the same as *ob*, and consequently *orb*, because *o* is interchangeable with *a* in occultism.

The Ever-Existent is identical to JHVH or Yahweh. JHVH is the Hebrew Tetragrammation or four-letter mystery name that was too sacred to be spoken. It was reversed as the name of the immutable "I Am." JHVH is common to theologies other than the Hebrew, and in the Egyptian mysteries was used as a password in the triliteral form of AUM or OM.

The youth is called the Fool because he, symbolizing superconsciousness, is beyond the understanding of self-consciousness or the intellectual mind. There is no thought, imagination, reasoning, feeling, or word to describe the state of superconsciousness. What men do not understand is often the object of ridicule. The fool is now the no-thing.

THE MEANING OF TAROT

The world thinks he is a fool because he does not concern himself with the ways of the world. Arcanum XXI comes before Arcanum XXII, the Universe (completion), for only after one returns to the beginning of existence, to innocence or holiness, is he complete. When the ego reaches this abyss, it will have completed the cycle of the Tarot, that is, the cycle of self-expression. But this is the beginning of an entirely new experience.

The Hebrew letter for Arcanum XXI is shin, the English sound for *sh*. It means "tooth." The numerical value is 300. This is the numeration of the Hebrew words RVCH ALHIM or *Rauch Elohim*, which in English means "Life-Breath of the gods" or "Spirit of God." Since Shin is the number of the Divine Spirit, the cabalists call it the Holy Letter.

DIVINATORY MEANING, UPRIGHT: In spiritual matters: idealism, originality, planning ahead, audacity, venturesome quest. In material matters: folly, eccentricity, nonconformity, inconsiderate action. The inquirer faces a choice in life of vital importance to him, requiring that he use all his powers to make the right choice. He is surrounded by strong spiritual forces. Therefore, rather than desiring perfection in the graces and attainments of society, he desires to adopt himself to a life of high and noble instincts. He wills to accomplish the highest point of spiritual attainment he can reach. Generally, this is the beginning of creativity. Since he is an individualist and does not conform to society's rules and patterns, he lives by his own beliefs in his climb above early regulation to a high future. Being his own man, apart from groups and regulations, he uses his own wisdom in seeking the adventure of life.

The Major Arcana

REVERSED: Foolish failure, likely to make faulty or foolish choices, too fearful to take chances; life will make a fool of him, will unhappily follow the established patterns and rules of society, the joy and possibilities of adventure will never be attained.

THE MEANING OF TAROT
ARCANUM XXII
THE UNIVERSE

A female figure is dancing within an oval wreath of laurel leaves. She is naked except for a flowing kaph-shaped scarf extending around her left shoulder and downward over the hips. Her female breasts are exposed, but the scarf covers her male properties. Thus she is both male and female.

Her arms extend down at right angles to the shoulders, and her left leg is crossing the right one. This position suggests the triangle over a cross, which is the sign of alchemical sulphur. In each hand she holds a spiraling wand. Each wand is rotating in opposite directions. The descending one in her left hand stands for involution, and the ascending one in her right hand stands for evolution. The wand in her right hand also represents the solar attraction, while the one in her left hand represents the lunar attraction.

The surrounding laurel wreath consists of twenty-two groups of three leaves, indicating that the twenty-two steps of the Tarot are now complete. The wreath is bound at the top and bottom with red bands of infinity symbols.

In the corners of the card are the heads of the four mystical animals, the Kerupic emblems, the Four Holy Living Creatures, the Four Holy Editors, the four Evangelists, the four animals of Apocalypse. Appearing at the upper right corner and moving clockwise are the heads of an eagle, a lion, a bull, and a man or angel, respectively. These are the same symbolic beings who were supporting the throne of JHVH (Yahweh) in Ezekiel's visons. These beings

The Major Arcana

are identical to the Chaldeo-Babylonian protecting genii (Cherubim) of the Babylonians and Assyrians. Later the four symbols were used in Christianity by St. John in his Apocalypse.

These four symbols have been used to represent a number of different manifestations of quaternaries. The Egyptian Sphinx is a representation of the four mystical symbols, for it has a human head, a woman's breast, the loins of a bull, the claws of a lion, and the wings of an eagle. The head represents intelligence, knowledge, and mystery; the claws, courage and action; the loins, will power, perserverance, strength, and labor; the folded wings, silence and inspiration. From this comes the Magi's quaternary of the Sphinx: to know, to dare, to will, to be silent.

According to hermetic philosophy, the parts of the Sphinx also represent the four elements of fire, water, earth, and air. Hence, the Sphinx represents the light of the stars and the properties of this light. The elements in their different combinations are the forms of the *Kingdom of Nature*.

The four mystic symbols have also been equated with the four Hebrew letters for the name of God, four seasons, certain signs of the Zodiac, and the four suits of the Minor Arcana. But the linkage of the four mystic symbols to the different manifestations of quaternaries varies from scholar to scholar.

The attributes of the designs of Arcanum XXII are the same as those of the corresponding leaf of the Egyptian Book of Thoth.

The infinity symbols binding the wreath, one above and one below, represent the macrocosm and the microcosm,

THE MEANING OF TAROT

the whole creation. The wreath, itself, symbolizes Nature on her regulated course. It is also the circle of completeness and perfection, the crown of those who master the four mystic animals or guardians and enter into the presence of the Dancer or unveiled Truth, thus obtaining perfect union with the One Power of the cosmos. The total picture of Arcanum XXII signifies Universal Cosmic Consciousness or what is known in Hindu philosophy as nirvana. In Arcanum XXI, the self-conscious intellect merged with the subconscious and blended into superconsciousness on the mountain peak. Then superconsciousness stepped out into the abyss, and in Arcanum XXII merged with Universal Cosmic Consciousness.

The Hebrew letter for this card is tav, which symbolizes perfection. The English sound or letter for tav is *T*. The numerical value is 400.

DIVINATORY MEANING, UPRIGHT: This is the card of Completion. Synthesis, completion of all things, reward, assured worldly success, happiness; rewards, the admiration of other, triumph in all undertakings; arrival at the state of cosmic consciousness; joy in living. It also can mean movement in one's affairs, travel, a voyage, change of place, escape, or change of residence.

REVERSED: Fear of change; earthbound spirit attached to one place or profession; sloth and stubborness; inertia, stagnation, refusal to learn the lessons of life as shown in the other cards; lack of vision; attachment to one place or profession.

Part Six

The Minor Arcana

THE secondary division of the Tarot, called the Minor Arcana or Lesser Arcana, consists of fifty-six illustrated cards, which are subdivided into four suits having fourteen cards each. The four suits are Wands (or Scepters), Cups, Swords, and Pentacles (or Coins).

The Wands suit corresponds to clubs in ordinary playing cards and indicates animation, enterprise, energy, growth, and glory. It represents both the business world of practicalities, social life, recreations, hobbies, and worldly glory.

The Cups suit corresponds to hearts and generally indicates love and happiness. It generally stands for peace and harmony and represents the inquirer's affections, relationships, family life, hopes, and joys.

The Swords suit corresponds to spades and indicates the threat of danger ahead, strife, misfortune, suffering, and a cruel, raw deal from fate. It also may represent the inquirer's public life, and his ambition, quest, thirst, driving force, aggression, degree of boldness and courage.

The Pentacles suit corresponds to diamonds and refers to money, interest, business, income, finances, and fortune

THE MEANING OF TAROT

in general. It represents the inquirer's material and financial attainment. Each letter of the holy name JHVH is represented by the Wands, Cups, Swords, and Pentacles respectively.

Each suit contains ten numbered cards, from Ace to Ten, and four Court cards of King, Queen, Horseman, and Attendant. The Court cards may represent either people (their thoughts) or their situations and modifying environmental influences.

The Kings may stand for a man and/or symbolize the spirit, which is the essential *self* in man.

The Queen may stand for a woman and/or symbolize the soul, which is the inner pattern of human personality.

The Attendant may represent a child of either sex and/or the body which is the personal vehicle of the individual spirit.

The Horseman may represent arrival or departure of a matter, and it may also represent the ego, which is the focus of energies and the personal sense of selfhood.

Whereas the Minor Arcana cards of most Tarot decks contain only emblematic designs, the deck used to describe the Minor Arcana in this book is illustrated with people in different life situations.

THE MINOR ARCANA—WANDS

King of Wands

Queen of Wands

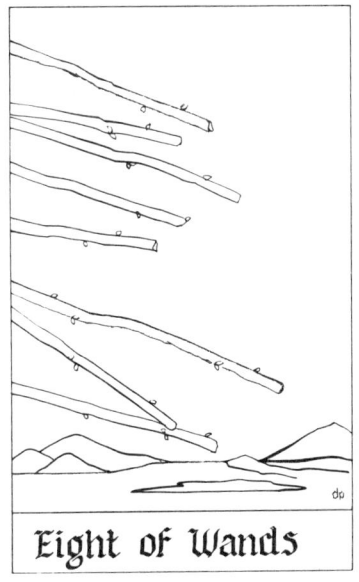

Four of Wands

Three of Wands

Two of Wands

Ace of Wands

The Minor Arcana

WANDS

The wands of all the Court cards are rough staffs sprouting occasional leaves.

KING OF WANDS

DESCRIPTION: The King is seated, in profile, upon a throne and holds a wand in his right hand. Both his robe and the high back of his throne are decorated with salamanders. The throne is also decorated with lions. In addition, a salamander rests on the base of his throne. The points of the King's crown are flame-shaped. It is uncertain whether the scene is an indoor or outdoor one.

DIVINATORY MEANING, UPRIGHT: Honesty. A dark-haired, friendly man living in the country; a country gentleman, usually married, honest, conscientious, loyal, devoted friend, well-balanced, mindful of the needs of others, ardent; knowledge; education; intelligence. This card always means honesty and may signify a good marriage. It may also signify an unexpected inheritance.

REVERSED: A man who is naturally good, but severe. Good but severe advice that should be heeded. An austere man, but tolerant to a degree. Counsel, advice, deliberation, high principles, exaggerated ideas of right and wrong, often ruthless if he has to be, tolerates people when it could bring him more harm than good.

QUEEN OF WANDS

DESCRIPTION: The exquisite Queen, wearing a crown and royal robes, sits on her throne in the open air with cone-shaped mountains in the background. She holds a wand in her right hand and a sunflower in the left. A carved lion forms each arm of her throne. The high back of her throne extending above her head is decorated with lions and sunflowers. A black cat is at her feet.

DIVINATORY MEANING, UPRIGHT: Life and Vitality. A dark, friendly, magnetic woman living in the country. This is always a card of life and vitality; loves home, loves nature, practical with money, good business sense, business success, quiet and wise person, philosophical, magnetic, domestic, charming, faithful, chaste, loving, honorable. But also love of money, greed, usury. If the card next to this one is a man, she feels favorably disposed toward him; if a woman, she has an interest in the inquirer.

REVERSED: A good, economical woman, strict, virtuous, obliging, and serviceable; may indicate good will toward the inquirer, but no opportunity to express it. But when this card is next to other cards with the same tendencies, it also signifies obstacles, resistance, opposition, jealousy, deceit, infidelity, emotional instability, untrustworthiness, lying.

HORSEMAN OF WANDS

DESCRIPTION: A Horseman in protective body-covering carries a short wand as he rides his light-colored horse in a hasty manner. His protective head-covering has a winged plume, and his surcoat is decorated with salamander designs. Mounds or pyramids and three cyprus trees, shaped like flames, are seen in the background. A road leads into the distance past a large stately residence or stronghold.

The Minor Arcana

DIVINATORY MEANING, UPRIGHT: Flight. A dark-haired, friendly, honest young man. Departure, absence and separation, disunion, flight, emigration, change of residence, journey, movement; sometimes may be a bad card, foretelling alienation.

REVERSED: Rupture, division, discord, interruption, quarrel, frustrated marriage, breaking up of a marriage or engagement; emotional problems interfering with work; refusal to give another person freedom.

ATTENDANT OF WANDS

DESCRIPTION: The Attendant stands in open country with cone-shaped mounds or pyramids and two cypress trees in the background. The trees are flame-shaped. The Attendant holds a wand, as though he were in the act of proclamation. He wears a sheathed knife at his belt and a hat with a flamelike plume. His dress is decorated with salamander designs. He is the eternal messenger.

DIVINATORY MEANING, UPRIGHT: A Message. A dark-haired young stranger; may represent a new lover who will enter a woman's life; a messenger who will bring good news or thoughts that are advantageous to the inquirer; a good man, faithful, a lover, pleasure, brilliance, courage, satisfaction. If this card is beside a man, the Attendant will bring favorable testimony concerning the inquirer. If this card is followed by the Attendant of Cups, it signifies a dangerous rival. Also, a young man with good family background looking for a mate.

REVERSED: Bad news, thoughts opposed to the interests of the inquirer, displeasure, anecdotes, announcements,

THE MEANING OF TAROT

feeling of trouble, worry; indecision and, consequently, instability; gossip.

TEN OF WANDS

DESCRIPTION: A man, bent under the weight of the bundle of ten wands he is carrying, walks toward a building in the background to the right.

DIVINATORY MEANING, UPRIGHT: This card has many different meanings: confidence, security, honor, good faith, invention, profit; excessive activity, work of genius, harvest, and travel. This card may indicate the problems of too much success; abundance of success which is oppressive or weighs down; acquiring of fortune, gain, success followed by the oppression of these things. This card may also represent falseness, disguise, perfidy; the wands the man is carrying may cause suffering to those he delivers them to; the card may represent heavy guilt from presenting a false appearance for gain, or it may indicate heavy worry or fear. Burden of badly regulated power.

REVERSED: A traitor, a liar, a person who will cause others great difficulties; contrariness, difficulties, intrigue, treachery, evasion, hindrance, or obstruction.

NINE OF WANDS

DESCRIPTION: A man with a headband or bandage around his head is holding a staff or wand in both hands as he stands on guard before eight wands which are upright and evenly spaced, forming what looks like a palisade.

The Minor Arcana

DIVINATORY MEANING, UPRIGHT: Preparedness. Means hidden enemies are near at hand, pending trouble; but the inquirer has reserve strength and alertness needed to overcome the trouble. Meets attack boldly, bravery in defense of himself, formidable antagonist, preparedness, strength in reserve; victory after opposition. Also means prudence and foresight, experience and lucky speculations; a period of rest from action. New friends, profitable friendships, but also could mean delay, suspension, adjournment. Order, discipline, good arrangement(s), disposition.

REVERSED: Delay, worry, disaster, obstacles, double-crosses, adversity, displeasure, calamity.

EIGHT OF WANDS

DESCRIPTION: Eight wands are shown across the card from top to bottom. The left ends of the wands extend out of sight beyond the left of the picture. Apparently in flight over open country, the right ends point toward the ground as though they are either just taking off or about to land.

DIVINATORY MEANINGS, UPRIGHT: Understanding, observation, direction, poise. Surroundings advantageous to life. Tact and diplomacy. Politics. The area of exchanges, commercial transactions; active undertakings, swiftness, great haste, great hope, speed toward happy goal, on the move. Also, arrows represent love.

REVERSED: Quarrels, discord. Arrows represent jealousy, internal disputes, stinging conscience, marital disputes.

SEVEN OF WANDS

DESCRIPTION: A young man stands on rolling ground very near the edge of a cliff, holding a flowering wand.

139

THE MEANING OF TAROT

He appears to be defending himself against the assaults of six others who are not shown in the picture. However, their flowering wands, which are raised up against him from the bottom of the cliff, are visible in the lower part of the picture.

DIVINATORY MEANING, UPRIGHT: Success, gain, advantage, profit, victory. Teaching, writing, publishing. Valor, intellectual discussion, worldly strife, invention, negotiations, trade war, barter, competition, courage in handling difficulties. Also means success.

REVERSED: Indecision, doubt, hesitation, embarrassment, anxiety. Perplexity, caution against indecision.

SIX OF WANDS

DESCRIPTION: A horseman riding a dark horse and wearing a laurel wreath of victory on his head carries a flowering wand also wreathed with laurel. Each of the five men on foot who accompany the horseman are holding up a flowering wand.

DIVINATORY MEANING, UPRIGHT: Has several different meanings. Laziness and work alternating. Attempt, hope, desire, wish, expectation, triumph, victory after strife, great news, hope, gain. Music, art, and drama.

REVERSED: Infidelity, treachery, disloyalty, faithlessness. Apprehension, fear of an enemy. Also means indefinite delay.

FIVE OF WANDS

DESCRIPTION: Five male youths appear to be in real or

mock combat with one another. Each is using a wand for a weapon.

DIVINATORY MEANING, UPRIGHT: Strife. Imitation, competition, and struggle for wealth and fortune. Also, a card of gold, gain, opulence, good business, betterment, heritage, riches fortune, money.

REVERSED: Legal proceedings, judgment, law, lawyer, tribunal. Litigation, disputes, trickery, contradiction.

FOUR OF WANDS

DESCRIPTION: Two maidens are carrying uplifted garlands behind a pavillion of four flowering wands with garlands suspended across their tops. Near the maidens and to the right of the picture is a bridge over a moat, leading to a large stately residence or stronghold in the background.

DIVINATORY MEANING, UPRIGHT: The coming of romance, harmony, prosperity, peace, intellectual fulfillment. The bounty of the harvest, home, perfected work, haven of refuge. Society, union, association, concord, harmony. Benefit or legacy.

REVERSED: Prosperity, success, happiness, advantage.

THREE OF WANDS

DESCRIPTION: A man with his back turned stands on a cliff at the top of a hill looking out at ships sailing on a large body of water. The man is surrounded by three wands planted in the ground. He is grasping the one on his immediate right.

THE MEANING OF TAROT

DIVINATORY MEANING, UPRIGHT: The beginning of a devotion to intellectual or commercial activity; established work. Trade, commerce, cooperation in business, partnership, practical help from a successful merchant. Enterprise, undertaking, commerce, trade, negotiation. Established strength, effort, discovery. Also able cooperation in business.

REVERSED: Beware of help offered. There may be treachery or at least disappointment. Hope, desire, attempt, wish. The end of troubles, suspension or cessation of adversity, toil, and disappointment.

TWO OF WANDS

DESCRIPTION: A man in fine attire looks out over the sea from the battlements of the tower of fortified residence. He holds a globe symbolizing the world in his right hand and a staff or wand in his left. The other wand in the picture is fixed in a ring to his right. A lily and a rose form a cross emblem on a battlement on the left.

DIVINATORY MEANING, UPRIGHT: Lord of the Manor. Wealth, fortune, magnificence, dominion. Interest in scientific methods or scientific activity. Riches, fortune, opulence, magnificence, grandeur. Alternative readings: riches, fortune, magnificence. Physical suffering, disease, chagrin, sadness, mortification.

REVERSED: Physical suffering, sadness, domination by others. Surprise, astonishment, event, extraordinary occurrence. Wonder, enchantment, emotion, trouble, fear.

ACE OF WANDS

DESCRIPTION: A hand appearing from a cloud holds a

wand with budding branches. The wand has ten leaves on it, while eight other leaves are falling to the ground. All of the leaves are shaped like yods. In the distance is a large stately residence or stronghold on top of a mountain.

DIVINATORY MEANING, UPRIGHT: Beginnings. Birth, commencement, origin, source, family. Powers of creation, invention and enterprise; energy, strength, principle. Maybe the starting of enterprises leading to money, fortune, inheritance. News of an opportunity.

REVERSED: Persecution, pursuit, violence, troubles, cruelty, tyranny. Fall, decadence, ruin, perdition; destruction or death. It can also mean an obscured joy.

CUPS

KING OF CUPS

DESCRIPTION: A King is sitting upon a throne near the sea. (Water is a symbol for the subconscious.) He holds a large cup in his right hand and a short lotus scepter (wand) in his left. The back of the throne is lotus-shaped and his crown is decorated with dolphins. A ship can be seen sailing in the background to the King's left and a dolphin is rising on his right.

DIVINATORY MEANING, UPRIGHT: A fair-haired man; kindness, goodness, generosity, liberality, calm exterior,

THE MEANING OF TAROT

responsible, at the inquirer's disposal. Also means artistic, scientific, fair; creative intelligence.

REVERSED: Dishonest man of good position, doubledealer; vice, roguery, injustice, execution, scandal, considerable loss, pillage, doubt, suspicion, distrust.

QUEEN OF CUPS

DESCRIPTION: A Queen in flowing robes sits by the seashore on a throne that is decorated with dolphins and crayfish. The top of the throne loops over her like a canopy, but it is in the shape of a dolphin's head. The clasp of the Queen's cloak is a small seashell. She is studying the ark-like shape of the large cup she holds in her hands. In the distance a ship can be seen.

DIVINATORY MEANING, UPRIGHT: Intelligence. A fair-haired, good, honest, devoted, woman will render service to the inquirer; imaginative, poetic. She symbolizes intelligence, the intuitive or clairvoyant mind; advantage, success and happiness in marriage; an excellent wife and mother, pleasure; also wisdom, virtue. But sometimes indicates a woman of equivocal character.

REVERSED: For a man, marriage into wealth; for a woman, distinguished but loveless marriage. Also, a woman of distinction who should not be trusted; a perverse woman; meddling, vice, dishonor, depravity. Success, but not without trouble.

HORSEMAN OF CUPS

DESCRIPTION: A Horseman holding a cup in his right hand is riding upon a white horse by the seashore. The

THE MINOR ARCANA—CUPS

King of Cups

Queen of Cups

Horseman of Cups

Attendant of Cups

Ten of Cups

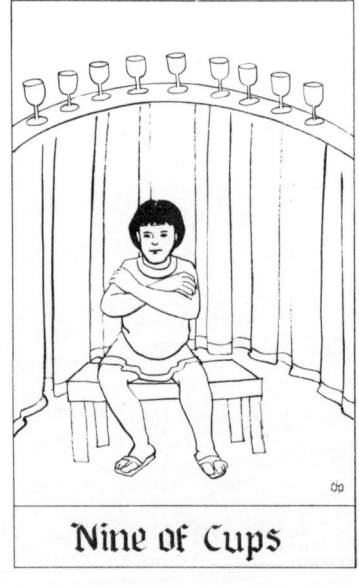
Nine of Cups

Eight of Cups

Seven of Cups

Six of Cups

Five of Cups

Four of Cups

Three of Cups

Two of Cups

Ace of Cups

The Minor Arcana

Horseman's headgear has wings on it, symbolic of imagination. His protective body-covering is decorated with dolphins and over his chest is a crayfish design.

DIVINATORY MEANING, UPRIGHT: Arrival. Approach of a messenger or an imaginative idea; a friend who will bring unexpected money. Advance(s), invitation, demeanor, incitement, a good business proposition. Also, indolent.

REVERSED: Deception, swindling, fraud, trickery, deceit, subtlety, hypocrisy, abuse of trust, cunning.

ATTENDANT OF CUPS

DESCRIPTION: An Attendant stands by the seashore looking at the fish rising from the cup in his right hand. The fish symbolizes the materialization of his imagination. The Attendant's coat is decorated with lilies, and the sheath of his dagger is decorated with dolphins. Behind the Attendant a dolphin jumps out of the sea.

DIVINATORY MEANING, UPRIGHT: Service. A fair-haired young man will be of service to the inquirer. Uprightness, discretion, confidence, integrity; news, message; meditation, application, reflection, contemplation, especially these things directed to business; a studious youth; a good omen.

REVERSED: Obstacles in your path; taste, inclination, attachment, seduction, deception, trickery, flatterer.

TEN OF CUPS

DESCRIPTION: A man and woman stand arm-in-arm hailing ten cups arranged side by side in the rainbow above. The area in the foreground where the man and woman stand is smooth and bare. Nearby, a little boy and girl are dancing together.

DIVINATORY MEANING, UPRIGHT: Contentment. Trust in one who is faithful and sincere, perfect love and friendship; honor, esteem, consideration, glory, virtue. For a male inquirer this card could indicate a good marriage surpassing all expectations. If this card is with several picture cards, it represents someone taking charge of the inquirer's interests; also, the inquirer's town or country. Lasting success; happiness to come.

REVERSED: Indignation, trust in one who is unfaithful and insincere, violence, combat, strife, serious quarrel, differences, opposition, dispute.

NINE OF CUPS

DESCRIPTION: A heavy, well-sustained man is sitting on a bench with his arms folded. Behind him a high curtain hangs from an arch. Nine cups support themselves around the arch. He is abundantly supplied for future sustenance.

DIVINATORY MEANING, UPRIGHT: Concord, contentment, physical well-being; also victory, triumph, material success, difficulties overcome, advantage, satisfaction. A good omen for men in military service.

REVERSED: Liberty, truth, loyalty; good business. It may also indicate mistakes, errors, imperfections, faults, however.

EIGHT OF CUPS

DESCRIPTION: A man with a staff in his right hand is walking desolately away from two rows of cups in the

The Minor Arcana

foreground, stacked three on top of five. Hills or jagged mountains protrude from a body of water which has cut inlets in the rocky terrain.

DIVINATORY MEANING, UPRIGHT: Joy, mildness, timidity, honor, modesty. Also means some affair previously thought to be important, whether good or bad, will decline in significance or have a diminished outcome. It may also indicate a fair-haired girl, marriage, friendship, tenderness, attachment. But it may mean abandoned success; instability. Leaving material success for something higher.

REVERSED: Happiness, great joy, feasting, perfect satisfaction, pleasure, gaiety.

SEVEN OF CUPS

DESCRIPTION: A man whose body and clothes are completely black stands with his back turned as he looks at the visions contained in seven cups resting on clouds in midair. The upright cups are arranged horizontally in two rows, with four cups on the bottom and three on the top. The cup on the extreme right of the top row, containing a snake, is raised a little higher than the others. The top left cup contains a man's head, while the middle cup contains a veiled, radiant figure. Starting from the left of the bottom row, the cups contain a stately residence on a hill, jewels, a wreath, and a winged serpent or dragon.

DIVINATORY MEANING, UPRIGHT: Illusions. Sentiment, imagination, reflected images, things seen in contemplation; ideas, designs, movement, resolutions. Illusionary success.

REVERSED: Will, determination, desire, plan, design,

THE MEANING OF TAROT

resolution, decision, project. If this card is accompanied by the Three of Cups, it indicates success.

SIX OF CUPS

DESCRIPTION: A little boy and a little girl stand in a small flower garden facing each other. The boy holds a cup they have filled with flowers. Four other filled cups are lined in a row on the ground across the bottom of the card, while still another filled cup stands on a pedestal behind the boy. The garden is in the yard of a house seen in the background.

DIVINATORY MEANING, UPRIGHT: Memories. Looking back on pleasant memories; happiness, enjoyment from the past. This card could indicate new relations, new knowledge, new environment, however. Beginning of steady gain, but a beginning only.

REVERSED: The future; renewal; something is coming soon.

FIVE OF CUPS

DESCRIPTION: A person in a dark cloak stands looking at the spilled contents of three overturned cups on the ground before his feet. Behind the person two cups remain upright on the ground. In the background to the right a bridge over a stream leads to a large residence or stronghold.

DIVINATORY MEANING, UPRIGHT: Inheritance, legacies, gifts, a heritage; transference, but not as expected; partial loss. It may also indicate a marriage, union, a joining. Also loss in pleasure; vain regret. It may indicate success in an enterprise.

REVERSED: Returning, arrival, alliances, news, surprise, ancestry, relationship. Also, false projects.

FOUR OF CUPS

DESCRIPTION: A discontented young man is sitting on the grass beneath a tree, his arms and legs crossed. To the left of the picture a hand from a cloud in midair offers the young man a cup. He does not seem to notice.

DIVINATORY MEANING, UPRIGHT: Aversion, weariness, boredom, disgust, imaginary troubles, displeasure, discontent; also, mixed pleasure. Contemplation. Dissatisfaction with material success.

REVERSED: New instruction, new acquaintance, new relations, novelty; presage; foreboding; conjecture; indication.

THREE OF CUPS

DESCRIPTION: Three maidens in flowing robes stand in a garden of fruit and foliage. Each raises her cup in a pledge of friendship.

DIVINATORY MEANING, UPRIGHT: Happy conclusion. Outcome of a matter; victory, triumph, success, fulfillment, healing, solace, pleasure, liberality. Also it can mean an unexpected promotion for a man in military service.

REVERSED: End of business, expedition, dispatch, achievement; cure; consolation.

THE MEANING OF TAROT
TWO OF CUPS

DESCRIPTION: A youthful male and a maiden, each wearing a wreath, stand in the open air holding cups toward each other in a mutual pledge. Between their cups rises the caduceus of Hermes or Mercury. At the top of the caduceus is a winged lion's head.

DIVINATORY MEANING, UPRIGHT: Love. Attachment, passion, friendship, affection, sentimental union, affinity; a work of love. Concord, sympathy, favorable pleasure, business; favorable love; also, wealth and honor. Reciprocity, reflection.

REVERSED: Opposition, obstacles, thwarted or frustrated desires, hindrance.

ACE OF CUPS

DESCRIPTION: A hand issuing from a cloud on the right supports a large cup the shape of which subtly suggests the Ark of the Covenant. Four streams gushing from the cup fall into a pool in which grow lotuses or water lilies. Several yods are falling as spray from the cup. At the top of the card a dove is descending into the cup.

DIVINATORY MEANING, UPRIGHT: Hospitality. A home of warmth, good cheer. A faithful, sincere, and loyal home. Happiness, joy, love, contentment, pleasure, beauty, nourishment, abundance, productiveness, fertility, banquet, feasting. Sometimes also indicates inflexibility, inflexible will, unchangeable law.

REVERSED: A faithless and deceitful home. Variable, alteration or transformation, change, instability, revolution. May also indicate an unexpected change of position.

SWORDS

KING OF SWORDS

DESCRIPTION: A stern-looking man is seated in the open air upon a throne that rests on a pavement of stone. The back of his throne extending above his head is a crescent moon and butterfly design. Trees are in the background. Appearing to be sitting in judgment, his right hand holds a sword and his left hand holds a book.

DIVINATORY MEANING, UPRIGHT: Power. A man with dark hair. He may represent the offices and power of the military, government, law, elected officials, judgment, etc. Power, counsel, command, superiority, authority.

REVERSED: An evil man or one with bad intentions. Worry, grief, fear, disturbance, perversity, faithlessness and disloyalty, cruelty. It may also be a warning to either be cautious in affairs that could result in a ruinous lawsuit or to halt a ruinous lawsuit.

QUEEN OF SWORDS

DESCRIPTION: A solemn-looking woman is seated in profile on a throne out-of-doors on a cloudy day. She looks straight ahead over the landscape. The throne is decorated with a winged child's head and butterfly emblems. The Queen's cape has clouds on it and her crown is decorated with butterflies. Her right hand holds a raised sword the hilt of which rests on the arm of her throne.

THE MEANING OF TAROT

DIVINATORY MEANING, UPRIGHT: A vivid, dark-haired woman of strong character. This card signifies loss, widowhood, womanly sadness, mourning, separation, embarrassment, absence, privation, sterility. It may also indicate a keen, quick, intensely perceptive, subtle, witty woman who usually likes to dance.

REVERSED: A bad woman, bearing malice toward the inquirer. Evil intent, bigotry, prudery, deceit, trickery, malice, ill-temper, narrow-mindedness, intolerance. It may also mean wealth, abundance, and joy mixed with discord, worry, and grief.

HORSEMAN OF SWORDS

DESCRIPTION: A Horseman rides headlong through the wind-swept countryside with his sword raised high. He wears a winged protective head-covering and protective body-covering decorated with a winged sphere. He is the picture of the gallant, mounted warrior.

DIVINATORY MEANING, UPRIGHT: Dominance. A dark-haired young man, soldier, or one who deals in arms, heroic action, bravery, skill, conflict, opposition, defense, or war. Active, clever, subtle, skillful, strong and domineering young man. Enmity, wrath, destruction, capacity, promptness, address, resistance, ruin. The cards immediately around this one in a spread should help to give the full meaning of the Horseman of Swords. It foretells a death only when it is near other death cards.

REVERSED: Imprudence, incapacity, extravagance, simplicity, ingeniousness, boasting; a conceited fool. It could also indicate a dispute with one who is stupid. If the inquirer is a woman, she will overcome a rival.

THE MINOR ARCANA—SWORDS

King of Swords

Queen of Swords

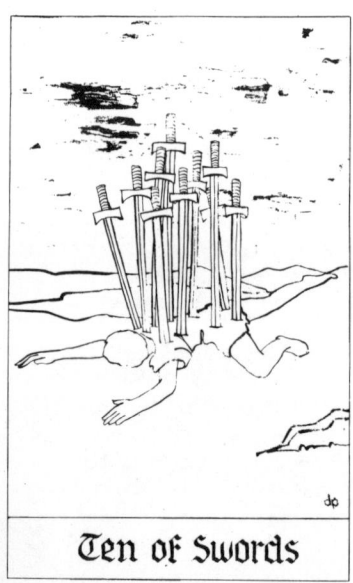

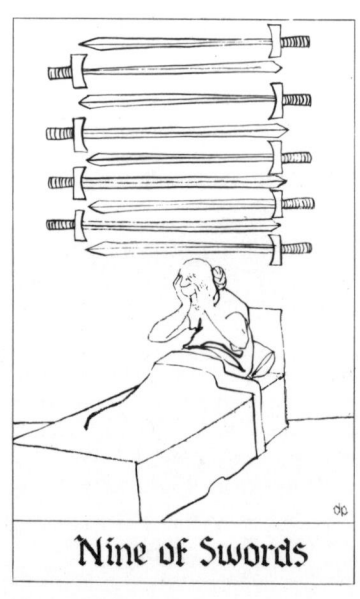

Eight of Swords

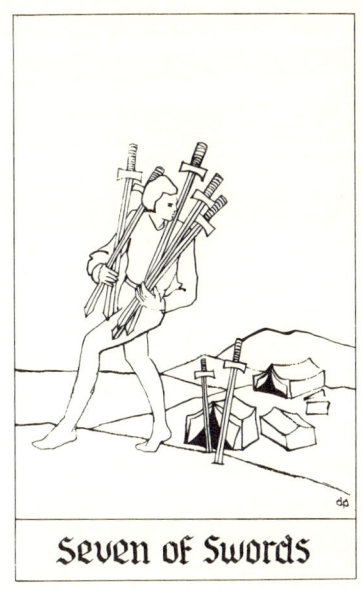

Seven of Swords

Six of Swords

Five of Swords

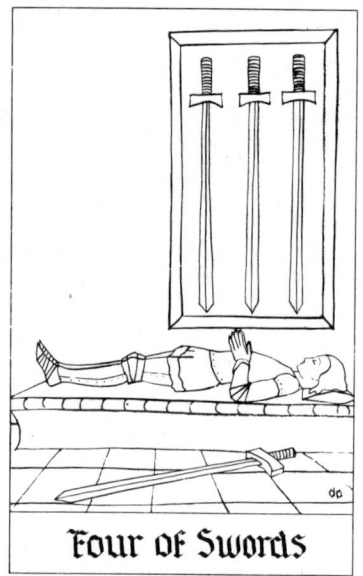

Four of Swords

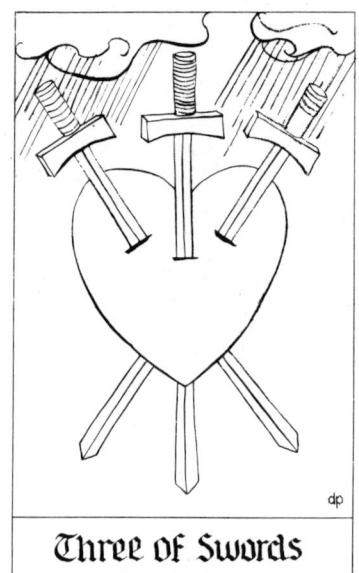

Three of Swords

Two of Swords

Ace of Swords

The Minor Arcana

ATTENDANT OF SWORDS

DESCRIPTION: An alert young Attendant holding a sword pointed upward with both hands is walking over rugged land. He looks over his shoulder as if he is expecting trouble or an attack. He wears a satchel at his waist. Many clouds are in the sky, and the wind is blowing his hair and the trees in the background.

DIVINATORY MEANING, UPRIGHT: Scrutiny. A dark-haired young man will pry into the inquirer's secrets; overseeing, secret service, spying (good or evil), searching, examining, A watchful, acute, subtle, active youth.

REVERSED: The more evil nature of the above qualities. The unknown, unforeseen events, unprepared state; watchful; supportive. It could mean sickness; or an imposter will probably be defeated.

TEN OF SWORDS

DESCRIPTION: A man lies prostrate on the ground with ten swords stuck into his body. The scene is desolate and the sky is dark.

DIVINATORY MEANING, UPRIGHT: Misfortune. Ruin, tears, affliction, grief, sorrow, burdens, sadness, pain, desolation. Not necessarily a card of sudden or violent death. In spiritual matters it means the end of delusion.

REVERSED: Temporary success, advantage, profit, power, and authority.

NINE OF SWORDS

DESCRIPTION: A woman is sitting up in bed holding her

THE MEANING OF TAROT

hands to her face in grief. Nine swords, one on top of the other, are placed behind her.

DIVINATORY MEANING, UPRIGHT: Failure, delay, misery, suffering, despair, deception, miscarriage, disappointment. It may also mean a death.

REVERSED: Suspicion, fear, doubt, distrust, shame, bad character, imprisonment.

EIGHT OF SWORDS

DESCRIPTION: A blindfolded woman with her arms bound to her sides is standing on watery, barren land surrounded by eight swords stuck into the ground. Five of the swords are on her left and three on her right. In the background a largely stately residence or stronghold can be seen on a high, rugged and otherwise barren hill.

DIVINATORY MEANING, UPRIGHT: Indecision; waste of energy in details. A crisis, sickness, criticism, blame, censure, bad news, conflict, slander, bondage; energy wasted on trifles.

REVERSED: Accident, treachery, disquiet, opposition, difficulty, incident, event.

SEVEN OF SWORDS

DESCRIPTION: A man carries three swords on his left shoulder and two on his right shoulder as he steals away from the tents of a military camp in the background. Holding the swords near the points, he looks over his left shoulder

The Minor Arcana

at the encampment and two other swords that remain behind stuck in the ground.

DIVINATORY MEANING, UPRIGHT: There are widely different meanings for this card: unstable effort; uncertainty; partial success, possible failure of a plan. Also, hope, attempt, design, wish, desire, confidence.

REVERSED: Wise advice, good counsel, prudence, wisdom, precaution, instruction.

SIX OF SWORDS

DESCRIPTION: A small, flat-bottomed boat carrying a woman, a child, and six upright swords with their points downward is being ferried across a smooth river by a man who is thrusting with a pole against the river bottom.

DIVINATORY MEANING, UPRIGHT: Success after anxiety; passage from difficulties; a journey by water, voyage, travel; an envoy or messenger.

REVERSED: Declaration, revelation, surprise, confession. It may also indicate a proposal of love. There is a possibility it could mean a stalemate, trapped in difficulties of the moment, or an unhappy outcome of an affair.

FIVE OF SWORDS

DESCRIPTION: Two defeated persons leave their swords lying on the ground and walk toward the large body of water in the background. In the foreground, the man who has conquered them looks on as he carries two swords pointed

THE MEANING OF TAROT

upward on his left shoulder, while his right hand holds another sword with its point resting on the ground. The sky is filled with storm clouds.

DIVINATORY MEANING, UPRIGHT: Defeat, loss, failure, slander, dishonor, mourning, sadness, affliction, trouble, destruction, degradation, dishonor.

REVERSED: Defeat, loss, failure, slander, dishonor, mourning, sadness, affliction, trouble, destruction, degradation, dishonor.

FOUR OF SWORDS

DESCRIPTION: A horseman lies at full length upon a tomb with his hands pressed together in an attitude of prayer. One sword lies beside his tomb, while three others are suspended in a frame over his head and breast. The points are downward toward the horseman.

DIVINATORY MEANING, UPRIGHT: Rest. Rest from strife or often illness; relief from anxiety; quietness, solitude, retreat, abandonment. It could also indicate exile but not death.

REVERSED: Economy, precaution, prudence, greed.

THREE OF SWORDS

DESCRIPTION: A heart is pierced by three swords. One sword is run straight down through the heart while the ones on either side of it are thrust diagonally toward the center. This pierced heart is a little-known magical symbol. Rain and clouds are in the background at the top of the card.

DIVINATORY MEANING, UPRIGHT: Sorrow, disappointment,

The Minor Arcana

tears. Delay, absence, separation, removal, rupture, quarrel, division, dispersion.

REVERSED: Error, misrule, confusion, disorder, loss, mental estrangement, distraction.

TWO OF SWORDS

DESCRIPTION: A blindfolded woman sits upon a bench with her back to a large body of water that has rocks in it. Her arms are crossed on her breast as she balances a diagonally-held sword upon each shoulder. A crescent moon is in the sky.

DIVINATORY MEANING, UPRIGHT: Balanced force, stalemate, temporary truce in quarrels; impotence, conformity, firmness, courage, valor. It may also mean friendship.

REVERSED: False friends, imposters; lies, treachery, hypocrisy, disloyalty.

ACE OF SWORDS

DESCRIPTION: A hand issuing from a cloud holds a sword. A crown encircles the sword near the point. Olive branches hang from one side of the crown and laurel branches from the other. Six yod-shaped tongues of flame are falling around the sword, signifying the descent of the spirit.

DIVINATORY MEANING, UPRIGHT: Invoked force; power, conquest; activity. Triumph, fertility, prosperity.

REVERSED: The same as above with undesirable or disastrous results; embarrassment, foolish and hopeless love, hindrance, obstacle(s), possible disaster and tyranny.

THE MEANING OF TAROT
PENTACLES

A pentagram is inscribed on every pentacle in this suit.

KING OF PENTACLES

DESCRIPTION: A King is seated upon a throne decorated with bull's heads. In his right hand he holds a scepter with a globe of the world fastened to the top. He rests his left hand upon an upright pentacle on his knee. His robe is decorated with many symbols of abundant fruit. The scene is out-of-doors for the throne is surrounded by fruit and plant growth. Behind the King, a fortified residence can be seen in the near background.

DIVINATORY MEANING, UPRIGHT: Bravery, a dark-haired man. Valor, courage, victory, success. Intelligent, good mathematician, steady, reliable, loyal friend, virile, affectionate lover, good husband; aptitude for business; sees the good side of a person, would sacrifice for his family, has firm ideas, holds to his philosophies, unselfish if not taken advantage of.

REVERSED: A vicious old man; a dangerous man. Vice, ugliness, weakness, corruption, temptation, extravagance, perversity, jeopardy, doubt, fear, danger.

QUEEN OF PENTACLES

DESCRIPTION: A Queen is seated upon a throne decorated with pomegranates and other fruits, ram's heads, and a cupid or head of a winged child. The scene is out-of-doors, for her throne is surrounded by a shelter of leafy branches bearing roses. The Queen studies the pentacle that she

THE MINOR ARCANA—PENTACLES

Horseman of Pentacles

Attendant of Pentacles

Ten of Pentacles

Nine of Pentacles

Eight of Pentacles

Seven of Pentacles

Six of Pentacles

Five of Pentacles

Four of Pentacles

Three of Pentacles

Two of Pentacles

Ace of Pentacles

holds upright in her lap. A rabbit plays nearby in the foreground.

DIVINATORY MEANING, UPRIGHT: A dark-haired woman, intelligent, charming, serious; presents from a rich relative. If the inquirer is a young man, this card means a rich and happy marriage; affluence, generosity, liberality, security. Sees more than is presented to view, good understanding of human nature, finds hidden truths, has dignified grace, supporter of freedom and liberty, friendly and loyal, very good wife, but moody. Opulence, generosity magnificence, security, liberty.

REVERSED: Sickness, evil, fear, suspicion, suspense, viciousness, mistrust, doubt.

HORSEMAN OF PENTACLES

DESCRIPTION: The horseman sits on a black horse that stands on a rolling, ploughed field. Both figures are attired in fine array. The Horseman is wearing protective body-covering and the horse is decorated with ornamental covering about the saddle and harness. The Horseman is observing the upright pentacle that he balances in his right hand.

DIVINATORY MEANING, UPRIGHT: Usefulness. A brown-haired young man of service, of useful discoveries; responsibility. Philosophical, educator, enjoys beauty and the good life. Utility, serviceableness, interest, good principles, a normal good life, laborious, patient, trustworthy, order, regulations, wisdom, economy; a quiet man.

REVERSED: Brave man out of work; idleness, stagnation,

THE MEANING OF TAROT

negligent, unemployed, discouragement. Narrow-minded, desires of material gain, dogmatic views, lack of understanding of others. Inertia, placidity, carelessness.

ATTENDANT OF PENTACLES

DESCRIPTION: The young Attendant is either standing or moving slowly on a road in open green countryside. He has flowers or flowerlike objects in his hat and wears a sheathed dagger at his belt. The Attendant is staring at the upright pentacle hovering just above his raised hands. In the background can be seen trees, a mound or mountain, and a large stately stronghold.

DIVINATORY MEANING, UPRIGHT: Study. A brown-haired youth; scholarship. Also news and the bearer of messages. Studious, formation of ideas and philosophies; offers advice—good or bad. Application, scholarship, reflection, rule, management; diligent, careful, deliberate; order; economy.

REVERSED: Luxury, degradation; unfavorable news. Rebelliousness, nonconformity, liberality, extravagant spending, waste.

TEN OF PENTACLES

DESCRIPTION: A man, woman, and little child stand just outside the passageway of an arched gate to a large stately house and grounds. The archway is emblazoned with a shield bearing the distinctive emblem of the residents. The man has his back turned, while the woman and child are facing a bearded old man who sits just outside the gate petting one of the two white dogs at his feet. The old

The Minor Arcana

man's robe is abundantly decorated with mystic signs and bunches of grapes. Ten pentacles are superimposed on the whole picture in an arrangement suggesting the cabalistic Tree of Life.

DIVINATORY MEANING, UPRIGHT: Honor, good faith, the acquisition of wealth, an inheritance, gain, riches, material prosperity, family matters, archives, extraction, the swelling of a family.

REVERSED: Bad news, loss, danger of robbery, chance, fatality, gambling, hazardous games, waste. Sometimes a gift, dowry, pension.

NINE OF PENTACLES

DESCRIPTION: A woman with a bird on her left wrist stands in a vineyard abundant with grapes. Nine upright pentacles, separated into two groups, are embedded on the grapevines in clear view. The three pentacles on her left are so arranged as to suggest a triangle that points either upward or downward. The other six pentacles to her right form two upward-pointing triangles, one on top of the other. The woman's right hand rests on the top pentacle as she faces outward. A large stately house can be seen in the background.

DIVINATORY MEANING, UPRIGHT: Safety in material possessions, material gain, foresight, wisdom, the accumulation of wealth, prudence, discretion, success, accomplishment, certitude, discernment, completion.

REVERSED: Storms, destruction or disruption of property or means of livelihood, danger of thieves, encroachment, roguery, deception, voided project, bad faith, trickery.

THE MEANING OF TAROT

EIGHT OF PENTACLES

DESCRIPTION: A craftsman with hammer and chisel sits on a bench in a clearing out-of-doors engraving a pentacle. Five engraved pentacles hang vertically, one above the other, on a tall board or post to the right. Another completed pentacle hangs from the side of the bench, while still another lies on the ground behind the man's foot. A house or village can be seen in the background.

DIVINATORY MEANING, UPRIGHT: A dark girl. Beauty, candor, chastity, innocence, modesty. Also work, employment, commission, craftsmanship, skill in craft work, business, and material affairs.

REVERSED: Hypocrisy, flattery, shifty, usury. Skill for cunning and intrigue. Also voided ambition, vanity, cupidity, exaction.

SEVEN OF PENTACLES

DESCRIPTION: A young man leaning on his hoe studies six pentacles attached to a leafy bush on his right, which may be fruitless grapevines. A seventh pentacle is attached to leafy stems between the man's feet. His labor should bear fruit.

DIVINATORY MEANING, UPRIGHT: Very contradictory meanings. Money, finance, treasure, gain, profit, business, barter; maybe altercation, quarrel. However, it may also indicate innocence, ingenuity, purgation, success unfulfilled; delay, but growth.

REVERSED: Anxiety, worry, disturbance, melancholy.

The Minor Arcana

SIX OF PENTACLES

DESCRIPTION: A merchant stands out-of-doors between two kneeling beggars. He holds scales in his left hand while he gives money to one of the beggars. Six pentacles are placed around the top sides of the card.

DIVINATORY MEANING, UPRIGHT: Presents, gifts, gratification. May also mean attention, vigilance; present time acceptable to prosperity, material, prosperity, philanthropy.

REVERSED: Desire, passion, longing, cupidity, envy, aim, jealousy, illusion.

FIVE OF PENTACLES

DESCRIPTION: Two beggars, a man and a woman, in a snowstorm pass under a lighted window on which five pentacles are inscribed. The man is on crutches and both are in ragged clothing. In outer darkness, they pass by the inner light.

DIVINATORY MEANING, UPRIGHT: Love. Affection, sweetness, harmony, natural liking or attraction, adjustment; love of wife, husband, lover, or mistress.

REVERSED: Disorder, chaos, ruin, discard, shameless immorality, imprudence.

FOUR OF PENTACLES

DESCRIPTION: A man, wearing a crown with a pentacle on top, encircles another pentacle against his chest with his hands and arms. Also under each foot is a pentacle. A city is in the background.

THE MEANING OF TAROT

DIVINATORY MEANING, UPRIGHT: Assurance of possessions, cleaving to possessions; gift, legacy, inheritance; earthly power; physical forces, skill in directing them. Also pleasure, gaiety, enjoyment, satisfaction.

REVERSED: Suspense, delay, opposition, obstacles, hindrances.

THREE OF PENTACLES

DESCRIPTION: A mason standing on a bench is working on a design of three pentacles above a double doorway of a church or monastery. The two monks who stand by watching hold the plan.

DIVINATORY MEANING, UPRIGHT: Nobility. Rank, power, aristocracy, dignity, elevation, reknown, glory, skill, construction; material increase; growth; financial gain.

REVERSED: Mediocrity, childishness, pettiness, weakness; also, children, youths.

TWO OF PENTACLES

DESCRIPTION: A young man in a tall, phallic hat is dancing with a pentacle in each hand. The pentacles are joined by an endless cord of the lemniscate figure, the symbol of infinity, shaped like a horizontal number 8. The loops of the 8 surround the pentacles. In the background, two ships ride the high waves of an undulating sea.

DIVINATORY MEANING, UPRIGHT: Gaiety, recreation, harmony in midst of change. But also, written messages or

The Minor Arcana

news in writing bring obstacles, agitation, trouble embroilment; worry, difficulties, embarrassment.

REVERSED: Enforced gaiety, simulated enjoyment, literal sense, handwriting, composition, letters of exchange, message.

ACE OF PENTACLES

DESCRIPTION: A hand, sticking out of a cloud, holds a pentacle. Below, there is a garden of lilies with a flowery arch leading to high mountains in the distance.

DIVINATORY MEANING, UPRIGHT: This may be the most favorable of all the Tarot Cards. It brings happiness, perfect contentment, ecstasy; good intelligence; triumph, prosperity, material gain, riches; also, quick intelligence, gold.

REVERSED: The evil side of wealth, bad intelligence. Also, money, help, gain, prosperity, and comfort, but without enjoyment.

GLOSSARY OF TERMS

Arcana: Secret or mysterious knowledge contained in occult symbols.

Court Cards: The royal cards. Kings, Queens, Horsemen, and Attendants.

Cups: Correspond to Hearts in a regular playing card deck.

Divination: The discovery of secret meaning or hidden knowledge through mysterious means.

Inquirer: The person for whom a Tarot spread is interpreted, or one who asks questions to be answered by the cards.

Major Arcana: Twenty-two cards symbolically representing esoteric truths, each with a different meaning. Sometimes known as "Trumps Major."

Minor Arcana: Four suits of 14 cards each, 4 Court cards and 10 numbered cards. Sometimes called Lesser Arcana. These suits are Wands (or Scepters), Cups, Swords, and Pentacles (or Coins).

Pentacle: A coin inscribed with a pentagram (five pointed star). Corresponds to Diamonds in the usual playing cards.

Reader: The interpreter of the meaning of the Tarot cards. A master of Tarot.

Significator: A Tarot card corresponding to the personal description of the inquirer, used to represent the person about which an inquiry is made.

Spread: An arrangement of the Tarot cards determined by the type of reading planned.

Swords: Corresponds to Spades in the usual playing card deck.

Tarot: The ancient, occult method of divination through interpretation of mysterious symbols.

Wands: Corresponds to Clubs in the usual playing card deck.